THE
Perfect
TURKEY

MORE THAN 100 MOUTHWATERING
RECIPES FOR THE ULTIMATE FEAST

The Perfect Turkey

13-Digit ISBN: 978-1-60433-806-5

10-Digit ISBN: 1-60433-806-7

This book can be ordered by mail from the publisher. Please include $5.99 for postage and handling. Please support your local bookseller first!

Books published by Cider Mill Press Book Publishers are available at special discounts for bulk purchases in the United States by corporations, institutions, and other organizations. For more information, please contact the publisher.

Cider Mill Press Book Publishers
"Where good books are ready for press"
PO Box 454
12 Spring Street
Kennebunkport, Maine 04046

Visit us online!
www.cidermillpress.com

Images by Keith Sarasin: pages 15, 19, 27, 87, 123, 124, 170, 173, 197, and 231.
All other images used under official license from Shutterstock.com.
Typography: Sentinel, Helvetica Rounded

Printed in China

1 2 3 4 5 6 7 8 9 0

First Edition

THE
Perfect
TURKEY

MORE THAN 100 MOUTHWATERING
RECIPES FOR THE ULTIMATE FEAST

KEITH SARASIN

CIDER MILL PRESS

BOOK
PUBLISHERS
KENNEBUNKPORT, MAINE

Contents

Introduction

The idea of the perfect turkey conjures many images in our mind, from golden skin to tender, moist breast meat. This ideal has proven elusive, making the turkey a dish that is feared by many and mastered by few.

To master the turkey, we must start at the farm. With this inside look, we can start to understand one of today's most over-looked proteins.

The turkey is native to the Americas and is believed to have been domesticated in Mexico. They have a strict social pecking order: the males, known as "toms," are flashy and colorful and display a much more aggressive attitude toward passersby than the females, known as "hens."

Domestic turkeys are bred to grow large for their meat, as opposed to the wild turkey, which is smaller with a gamier flavor. In the wild, turkeys forage for insects, seeds, and the occasional frog. Wild turkeys can fly for short distances and like to keep to wooded areas for foraging purposes.

Understanding the differences between domestically grown birds and wild or free-range farm turkeys gives us insight on how to prepare the turkey. Domestically grown turkeys are fed grain to increase their size in a short time as opposed to free-range farm turkeys, which are supplemented with grain but depend on a foraged diet like their wild brothers and sisters.

Because of this, the method for cooking a free-range turkey as opposed to a domestically grown turkey changes a bit. When I cook a free-range turkey, I like to sear the bird in the oven at 425°F for about 15 to 20 minutes to render the fat. Then, I lower the heat to 325°F and cover and cook the bird. When you render the fat of the bird this way, you draw out the meat's inherently rich flavor.

The other caveat to cooking a free-range bird is the brine. Domestically grown turkeys are almost always injected with some type of sodium solution to prevent the meat from drying out. Free-range birds do not receive these injections and as such benefit greatly from a brine, which helps moisten and protect the meat.

Bottom line, whether you are buying a domestically grown bird or a free-range one, turkey is fantastic when correctly prepared.

One of the major roadblocks we face when we think about turkey is the oven. By fixating on the oven as the primary cooking method for turkey, we often overlook other ways to cook the bird, like in the smoker or on the grill. Throughout this book, we highlight methods, spices, flavor profiles, and sides that will open your eyes to the versatility of turkey. From rubs to wet brines, dry brines to sides, creating the perfect turkey is finally at your fingertips.

The goal of this book is to expand your horizons and make turkey a mainstay on your dinner table. Follow the advice in this book, and you'll find that turkey has the potential to transform meals other than Thanksgiving dinner.

Preparing a Turkey

How to Thaw a Turkey

Remember to keep the turkey inside the packaging while thawing.

The safest method to properly thaw a turkey is by allowing it to sit in the refrigerator for a few days. It will take about 24 hours per 5 pounds of turkey to thaw in the fridge. To do this, place the turkey on a large baking sheet and slide it into the fridge

The second method requires thawing the turkey in cold water, which can take anywhere from 20 to 30 minutes per pound of turkey to fully thaw. With this method, you need to be sure to rotate and flip the turkey, as well as change out the water every 30 minutes to make sure that the whole turkey remains cold.

Trussing a Turkey

One of the most important parts of cooking a whole turkey is learning to properly truss it. This task may seem overwhelming at first, but it is very simple. Trussing a whole bird allows the bird to maintain its shape and ensures that it cooks evenly.

STEP 1: TOOLS

- A thawed turkey
- A sanitized surface
- Kitchen twine
- Kitchen shears

STEP 2: TRUSSING

- Cut a piece of kitchen twine that is 48 to 52 inches long.
- Pat the bird dry and place it in front of you with the legs pointed toward you.
- At the center point of the piece of twine, wrap the twine around the neck of the turkey and make a small knot.
- Bring the twine under the turkey to the wings. Then, tuck the wings under the turkey and wrap the twine around the wings.
- Take the twine, pull it tightly under the breast near the cavity of the bird and make a tight knot.
- Bring the legs together and tie them tight.
- Remove any extra string.

Cooking a Turkey

Cooking a Turkey

Traditional Oven-Roasted Turkey

SERVES: 5 TO 10 DEPENDING ON SIZE
ACTIVE TIME: 30 MINUTES • TOTAL TIME: 3 TO 5 HOURS

This oven roasting method brings simple aromatics to the bird without masking its flavor.

1 Preheat oven to 450°F.

2 Halve the lemon and onion and sear them facedown in a hot pan until they are darkened.

3 Remove the giblets from the cavity of the turkey. Save them for gravy .

4 Rinse the cavity and outside of the turkey with cold water. Pat the entire bird dry.

5 Place the seared onion, lemon, and the sage leaves into the cavity of the turkey.

6 Slice a small slit in the skin of the breast, being careful not to puncture the meat.

7 Using your index finger, separate the skin from the meat, being careful to keep the skin intact. Carefully place 5 tablespoons of butter between the skin and meat.

8 Rub the salt all over the outside of the turkey. Place the turkey in an oven-safe dish and tent it with foil or cover it with a lid.

INGREDIENTS

1 lemon

1 medium sweet onion

1 10 to 20 lb. turkey

4 to 6 sage leaves

5 tablespoons butter

2 teaspoons salt

9 Place in the oven and cook for 30 minutes.

10 After 30 minutes, turn the oven down to 350°F and cook for 2 to 4 hours, depending on size.

11 Check the temperature of the breast with a thermometer. Before it reaches 155°F, raise the oven temperature to 450°F for about 10 minutes to brown the skin. .

NOTE: Stuffing a bird is not only risky because of pathogens, it also dries out the bird. If you want the classic stuffing presentation at the table, do it after the bird is done.

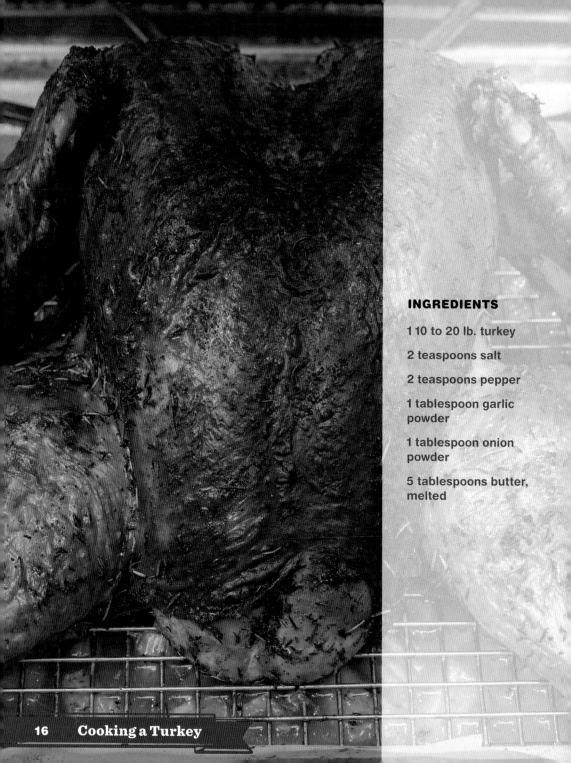

INGREDIENTS

1 10 to 20 lb. turkey

2 teaspoons salt

2 teaspoons pepper

1 tablespoon garlic powder

1 tablespoon onion powder

5 tablespoons butter, melted

Spatchcocked Turkey

SERVES: 5 TO 10 DEPENDING ON SIZE • ACTIVE TIME: 30 MINUTES
TOTAL TIME: 1 HOUR AND 25 MINUTES TO 2 HOURS

Typically, the legs and the breast of a turkey have two different ideal temperatures. The spatchcock method solves this by flattening the bird so it cooks evenly.

1 Preheat oven to 450°F.

2 Place turkey breast side down on a cutting board.

3 Take a pair of kitchen shears, cut along each side of the turkey's backbone, and remove the backbone.

4 Flip the turkey back over so the breast side is up.

5 Place the turkey in a pan with a wire rack.

6 Push down on the middle of the bird to flatten it as much as possible.

7 Rub the melted butter all over the breast.

8 Mix the salt, pepper, garlic powder, and onion powder together.

9 Rub the salt mixture over the breast.

10 Cook the turkey uncovered until the breast reads 155°F and the legs are at least 165°F, about 1 hour to 1 hour and 25 minutes.

Smoked Turkey

Smoking a whole turkey might seem like a big task, but it is one of the tastiest ways to prepare a bird. When smoking a turkey, cook at a low temperature (235°F to 250°F) for about 30 minutes a pound, or you can cook it at a higher temperature, as this tends to yield a crisper skin. If you want to go with the lower temperature, finish the turkey in an oven at 450°F for 7 to 10 minutes to crisp the skin. For wood options, apple, cherry, and hickory all give the turkey a sweeter flavor.

INGREDIENTS

1 12 to 20 lb. turkey

Rub of choice

3 cups of water

1 Soak wood for 1 hour before using. This allows the smoke to dissipate slower.

2 Preheat the smoker to 250°F.

3 Pat the inside and outside of the turkey dry and use your favorite rub.

4 Add the water to the steam tray in your smoker.

5 Place an aluminum drip pan on the grate below your bird to catch the drippings.

6 Place the turkey on a rack above your drip pan. Add about 8 oz. wood to the smoker and close.

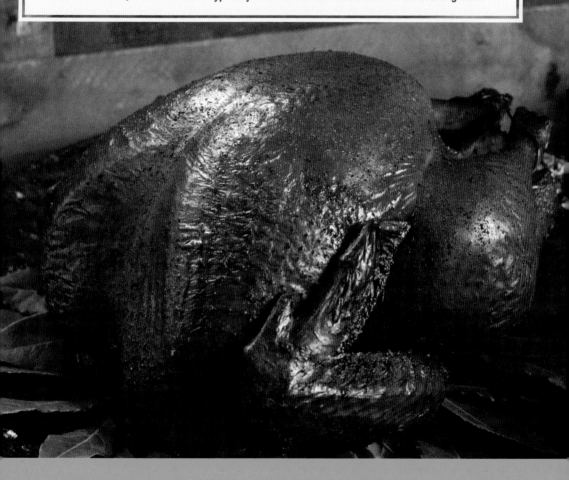

7 Smoke for 6 to 10 hours, making sure to add water to steam pan and wood as needed. When the internal temperature of the breast reaches 165°F, remove the turkey, wrap in foil, and allow to rest for 15 to 20 minutes.

Deep-Fried Turkey

Deep frying a turkey yields incredibly crispy skin while leaving juicy, tender meat. This method is quick but requires a lot of caution and cleanup.

INGREDIENTS

1 10 to 20 lb. turkey (innards removed)

2 teaspoons salt or rub of choice

3 gallons peanut oil

1 Pat the turkey inside and out to get it as dry as possible.

2 Rub the salt or your favorite rub over the outside of the bird.

3 Heat turkey fryer oil to 350°F. Make sure you leave plenty of room for the turkey so that the oil doesn't spill over.

4 Place the turkey in the fryer basket. Lower the basket into the oil until the turkey is covered.

5 Keep the oil at 350°F, adjusting the temperature as needed. Cook the turkey for 3 minutes per pound.

6 Carefully remove the basket from the oil and place turkey on a towel-lined platter to drain.

7 Insert a meat thermometer into the leg. The turkey is done when the temperature reaches 180°F.

NOTES:

Deep frying a turkey is very dangerous and needs to be done carefully.

- Only fry a turkey outside

- Do not allow children or pets around the fryer

- Use a proper turkey fryer and read the instructions before starting

- Never leave the fryer unattended

- Never fry a frozen turkey

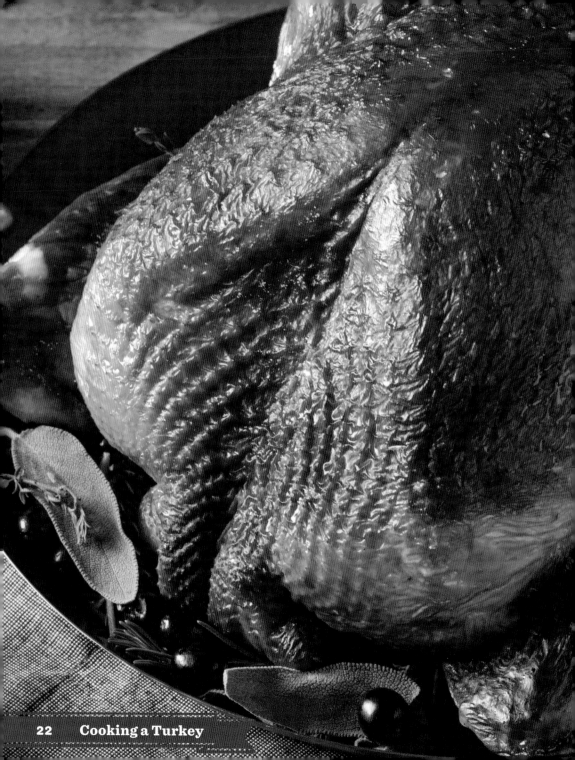

Grilled Turkey

Grilling allows you to free up your oven for all the side dishes you want to cook and adds a nice smoky flavor to the turkey.

1 Pat the inside and outside of the turkey dry.

2 Have your rub ready and work into the inside and outside of the bird. Stuff with the aromatics.

3 Tuck the wing tips under the breast of the turkey and truss the legs together (see page 10).

4 Heat your grill on high for 10 minutes, then turn off one of the burners.

5 Place the turkey in a pan with 2 cups of water. Then, place the pan containing the turkey on the grill grate that is turned on.

6 Close the grill cover and maintain a temperature of 450°F until the legs of the turkey register 170°F.

INGREDIENTS

1 10 to 20 lb. turkey (innards removed)

Rub of choice

1 lemon, quartered

1 onion, quartered

2 sprigs sage

2 sprigs thyme

2 springs rosemary

Spatchcocked Grilled Turkey

**SERVES: 5 TO 10 DEPENDING ON SIZE • ACTIVE TIME: 25 MINUTES
TOTAL TIME: 8 TO 14 HOURS**

This method yields a tasty, slightly smoky turkey in relatively little time.

INGREDIENTS

1 10 to 20 lb. turkey

Rub of choice

1 Remove the innards and backbone as you do in the conventional spatchcock method (see page 17).

2 Use your favorite rub recipe and massage the rub into the turkey.

3 Place bird on a wire rack uncovered in the fridge for 6 to 12 hours before you cook it.

4 Heat your grill on high for 10 minutes, and then turn off one of the burners.

5 Place the turkey breast side up in a pan with 2 cups of water. Cover and place the pan containing the turkey over the burner that is turned on.

6 Close the grill cover and maintain a temperature of 350°F.

7 About halfway through the cooking time, remove the cover and continue to cook until the thickest part of the leg registers 165°F.

8 Remove pan from the grill, tent with foil, and allow to rest for 20 minutes.

Sous Vide Turkey

SERVES: 5 TO 10 DEPENDING ON SIZE
ACTIVE TIME: 50 MINUTES • TOTAL TIME: 24 HOURS

Sous vide translates as "under vacuum" and consists of cooking food at a very precise temperature.

The food is typically put into a plastic pouch or glass jar and cooked in a water bath for food that is juicy, tender, and evenly cooked.

Once you sous vide a turkey, you will never look back.

1 Bring your immersion circulator to 150°F 24 hours before you want to serve the turkey.

2 Break down the turkey. Then cut the breast into two pieces.

3 Apply the rub and place the breasts into one bag and the legs into another.

4 Place the bag with the legs into the water, making sure to get all the air out as you submerge them.

5 Place the bag with the breasts into the fridge. After 12 hours, lower the temperature on the immersion calculator to 133°F.

6 Add the bag of turkey breasts to the water and continue to cook for 12 more hours, making sure to get all the air out as you submerge the turkey breasts.

7 Remove the bags of turkey 30 minutes before you are ready to eat.

8 Put a pan on the stove and warm over medium-high heat.

NOTE: You will want to brine your turkey and have it ready to go the day before you want to eat it. Typical cooking time for the legs is 24 hours at 133°F. You can cook them quicker if you raise the temperature to 168°F, but the method we highlight in the directions yields the best flavor.

9 Remove the turkey from the bags and pat dry. Salt the turkey.

10 Add the oil to the hot pan. Sear the legs skin side down until golden brown, about 3 to 5 minutes.

11 Flip the legs. Using a spoon, baste the legs for 3 minutes until golden. Repeat this step with the turkey breasts and serve.

INGREDIENTS

1 10 to 20 lb. turkey, thawed and broken down into legs and breast

Rub of choice

1 tablespoon salt

3 tablespoons oil

Brined and Grilled Turkey

SERVES: 6 • ACTIVE TIME: 3 HOURS • TOTAL TIME: 9 TO 24 HOURS

Brining and grilling poultry often go hand in hand, as it allows the meat to retain its juices.

INGREDIENTS

12 to 14 lb. turkey

8 cups cold water

½ cup kosher salt

2 oranges, halved

2 tablespoons clarified butter

Black pepper, to taste

½ sprig rosemary, leaves removed

1 In a large stockpot, add the turkey and submerge in the water and kosher salt. If more water is needed, add more kosher salt proportionately. Let the turkey brine at room temperature for 6 to 12 hours.

2 Remove the turkey and pat dry. Squeeze the juice of the orange halves over the turkey and inside the cavity. Rub the clarified butter on the turkey's skin and season with black pepper and rosemary.

3 Heat a gas or charcoal grill to medium-low heat and designate two separate heat sections on the grill, one for direct heat and the other for indirect. To control the heat, arrange the coals on one side of the grill or turn off one of the burners.

4 When the grill is about 350°F to 400°F, place the turkey over indirect heat and grill for about 2 hours and 45 minutes. Replenish the coals and flip the turkey every 45 minutes. Insert a meat thermometer into the thickest part of the thigh. The turkey is finished when the thermometer reads 165°F.

5 Remove the turkey from the grill and cover with aluminum foil. Let rest for 45 minutes to 1 hour before carving.

Cajun Turkey with Cranberry Sauce

SERVES: 6 TO 8 • ACTIVE TIME: 3 HOURS • TOTAL TIME: 10 TO 24 HOURS

Combining the sweetness of the cranberry sauce with the added heat from the Cajun turkey creates an unforgettable pairing.

1 Place the turkey in a large stockpot. Submerge in the water and kosher salt. Add more water as needed, increasing kosher salt proportionately. Let the turkey brine at room temperature for 6 to 12 hours.

2 For the cranberry sauce, combine the cranberries, honey, orange juice, and lemon juice in a medium saucepan and cook over medium heat. Simmer for about 15 minutes, until the sauce thickens and the berries have broken apart. Transfer to a bowl and refrigerate overnight.

3 Remove the turkey from the brine and pat dry. In a small bowl, mix the spices and herbs together. Spoon the clarified butter over the turkey and distribute evenly. Then, rub the spice mixture over the turkey. Let rest at room temperature for 1 to 2 hours.

4 Preheat your gas or charcoal grill to medium-low heat and designate two separate heat sections on the grill, one for direct heat and the other for indirect. To control the heat, arrange the coals toward one side of the grill or turn off one of the burners.

CAJUN TURKEY INGREDIENTS

12 to 14 lb. turkey

8 cups cold water

½ cup kosher salt

2 tablespoons clarified butter

2 tablespoons onion powder

2 tablespoons paprika

1 tablespoon cayenne pepper

1 tablespoon garlic powder

1 tablespoon ground oregano

1 tablespoon dried thyme

1 tablespoon coarsely ground black pepper

1 tablespoon fresh sea salt

CRANBERRY SAUCE INGREDIENTS

4 cups raw cranberries

½ cup honey

½ cup orange juice

Juice from ½ small lemon

5 When the grill reaches 350° to 400°F, place the turkey over indirect heat and grill for 2 to 2½ hours. Replenish the coals and flip the turkey every 45 minutes. Insert a meat thermometer into the thickest part of the thigh. The turkey should be at 165°F when finished.

6 Remove the turkey from the grill and cover with aluminum foil. Let rest for 45 minutes to 1 hour before carving. Serve alongside cranberry sauce.

Carving a Turkey

Carving a Turkey

How to Carve a Turkey

Allow turkey to rest for 20 to 30 minutes after it has finished cooking to ensure that the juices seep into the meat. Reserve the pan drippings for your gravy.

Begin by removing any twine that you may have used to truss the turkey. Then, carefully transfer the turkey to a carving board.

Make sure that you have a stable surface to work on while carving and that you use a sharp knife.

Start by removing the legs. Place your knife on the area of skin that joins the drumstick to the breast. Slice through the connective area until you reach the joint. From there, press down until you hear a click, signaling that the joint has come out of the socket.

Next, use the knife to finish cutting through the bottom side of the thigh. Do this same process for both legs. Remove the meat from the bone and slice into serving portions. Transfer to a serving platter.

You may want to remove the wishbone before carving the breast meat. This makes it easier to carve, but is not a necessary step. Find the wishbone at the front of the breast and slide your fingers in. Pull to remove.

Place your knife on either side of the breast plate and slice along the bone, keeping your knife as close to the bone as possible to make sure to get the maximum yield. While slicing down, use your free hand to pull the meat away from the carcass. Repeat this step on the opposite side.

Lay each breast flat and locate the joint connected to the wing. Carve around the joint and transfer to the serving platter.

Once wings are removed, slice the breast horizontally, being careful not to tear the skin off. Transfer to the serving platter.

Brines

Traditional Dry Brine

YIELD: BRINE FOR 10 TO 20 LB. TURKEY
ACTIVE TIME: 10 MINUTES • TOTAL TIME: 24 HOURS

This traditional dry brine is all about the herbs and adds a wonderful, classic flavor to any turkey, while still preserving the moisture you want in the bird.

1 Remove the turkey from its packaging and remove the innards. You can reserve these for gravy. Rinse the turkey under cold water and dry it with a towel.

2 Combine all ingredients together and mix thoroughly.

3 Rub mixture under the turkey skin, all over the outside, and inside the carcass.

4 Cover with foil and place in the refrigerator for 24 hours.

INGREDIENTS

5 tablespoons unsalted butter, melted

1 tablespoon salt

1 tablespoon pepper

1 tablespoon sugar

1 tablespoon sage

1 tablespoon rosemary

1 tablespoon thyme

2 teaspoons paprika

1 tablespoon garlic powder

Roasted Vegetable Brine

YIELD: BRINE FOR 10 TO 20 LB. TURKEY
ACTIVE TIME: 55 MINUTES • TOTAL TIME: 25 HOURS

This wet brine adds a deep, rich flavor to any turkey and it's a great way to use up vegetable scraps.

INGREDIENTS

5 cups vegetable scraps

2 tablespoons sugar

2 tablespoons salt, plus more to taste

½ cup peppercorns

5 bay leaves

¼ cup whole cloves

1 Remove the turkey from its packaging and remove the innards. You can reserve these for gravy. Rinse the turkey under cold water and dry it with a towel.

2 Cut the vegetable scraps into smaller pieces, season with salt, and char them in the oven until they are dark brown.

3 Add all of the ingredients along with the roasted vegetable scraps to the container you are brining the turkey in. Add the turkey and fill with enough water to fully submerge the turkey.

4 Place the turkey in the brine breast side down. Make sure that the turkey is fully submerged, weighing down with plates if necessary. Refrigerate for 24 hours.

5 Remove the turkey from the brine and dry the bird inside and out. Discard the brine and cook the turkey.

40   Brines

Sweet and Smoky Dry Brine

YIELD: BRINE FOR 10 TO 20 LB. TURKEY
ACTIVE TIME: 10 MINUTES • TOTAL TIME: 24 HOURS

This dry brine combines sweet and smoky flavors for a tasty new way to enjoy your turkey, complementing the flavor without masking it.

INGREDIENTS

2 tablespoons salt

2 tablespoons pepper

¼ cup brown sugar

3 tablespoons paprika

1 tablespoon garlic powder

1 tablespoon onion powder

2 teaspoons lemon zest

1 Remove the turkey from its packaging and remove the innards. You can reserve these for gravy. Rinse the turkey under cold water and dry it with a towel.

2 Combine all ingredients together and mix thoroughly.

3 Rub mixture under the turkey, all over the outside, and inside the carcass.

4 Cover the turkey with foil and place in the refrigerator for 24 hours.

Cranberry Brine

YIELD: BRINE FOR 10 TO 20 LB. TURKEY
ACTIVE TIME: 10 MINUTES • TOTAL TIME: 24 HOURS

This wet brine is a wonderful way to sweeten the turkey meat as well and add tenderness and flavor. This brine works particularly well on smoked turkey.

1 Remove the turkey from its packaging and remove the innards. You can reserve these for gravy. Rinse the turkey under cold water and dry it with a towel.

2 Add all of the ingredients to the container you are brining the turkey in and stir to combine. Add the turkey and fill with enough water to fully submerge the turkey.

3 Place the turkey in the brine breast side down. Make sure that the turkey is fully submerged, weighing down with plates if necessary. Refrigerate for 24 hours.

4 Remove the turkey from the brine and dry the bird inside and out. Discard the brine and cook the turkey.

INGREDIENTS

5 cups whole cranberries

3 cups cranberry juice

2 tablespoons salt

½ cup sugar

5 bay leaves

¼ cup whole cloves

1 orange, cut into slices

1 cup cranberry juice

2 tablespoons peppercorns

Maple Brine

YIELD: BRINE FOR 10 TO 20 LB. TURKEY
ACTIVE TIME: 10 MINUTES • TOTAL TIME: 24 HOURS

Maple adds a sweetness to turkey that is remarkable. For this dry brine, maple sugar helps preserve the tenderness of the turkey.

INGREDIENTS

- ¾ cup maple sugar
- 2 tablespoons salt
- 2 teaspoons pepper
- 2 teaspoons lemon zest
- 2 teaspoons paprika
- ½ teaspoon cinnamon
- ½ teaspoon nutmeg

1 Remove the turkey from its packaging and remove the innards. You can reserve these for gravy. Rinse the turkey under cold water and dry it with a towel.

2 Combine all ingredients together and mix thoroughly.

3 Rub mixture under the turkey skin, all over the outside, and inside the carcass as well.

4 Cover the turkey with foil and place in the refrigerator for 24 hours.

Apple Cider Brine

YIELD: BRINE FOR 10 TO 20 LB. TURKEY
ACTIVE TIME: 10 MINUTES • TOTAL TIME: 24 HOURS

This wet brine adds a tangy and sweet flavor to turkey and works particularly well with smoked preparations.

1 Remove the turkey from its packaging and remove the innards. You can reserve these for gravy. Rinse the turkey under cold water and dry it with a towel.

2 Add all of the ingredients to the container you are brining the turkey in and stir to combine. Add the turkey and fill with enough water to fully submerge the turkey.

3 Place the turkey in the brine breast side down. Make sure that the turkey is fully submerged, weighing down with plates if necessary. Refrigerate for 24 hours.

4 Remove the turkey from the brine and dry the bird inside and out. Discard the brine and cook the turkey.

INGREDIENTS

5 cups apple cider

2 tablespoons salt

3 bay leaves

1 tablespoon whole cloves

3 apples, cut into slices

4 cinnamon sticks

1 teaspoon nutmeg

Citrus Brine

YIELD: BRINE FOR 10 TO 20 LB. TURKEY
ACTIVE TIME: 40 MINUTES • TOTAL TIME: 24 HOURS

Tangy, sweet, and delicious is the best way to describe this wonderful citrus brine. For this wet brine, we use a variety of citrus to help layer flavors and preserve the tenderness of the turkey.

1 Remove the turkey from its packaging and remove the innards. You can reserve these for gravy. Rinse the turkey under cold water and dry it with a towel.

2 Add all of the ingredients to a pot of water and bring to a boil. Reduce heat and simmer for 20 minutes.

3 Remove from heat and allow the mixture to cool completely.

4 Place the turkey in the brine breast side down. Make sure that the turkey is fully submerged, weighing down with plates if necessary. Refrigerate for 24 hours.

5 Remove the turkey from the brine and dry the bird inside and out. Discard the brine and cook the turkey.

INGREDIENTS

1 cup sugar

¾ cup salt

2 lemons, cut into wedges

2 oranges, cut into wedges

2 limes, cut into wedges

5 bay leaves

2 cinnamon sticks

4 garlic cloves

Holiday-Spiced Wet Brine

YIELD: BRINE FOR 10 TO 20 LB. TURKEY
ACTIVE TIME: 45 MINUTES • TOTAL TIME: 24 HOURS

These iconic fall spices are a wonderful way of imparting a warm flavor to your next turkey without sacrificing any tenderness.

INGREDIENTS

¾ cup sugar

½ cup salt

5 bay leaves

3 cinnamon sticks

4 garlic cloves

3 sprigs thyme

3 sprigs rosemary

2 teaspoons cloves

2 teaspoons nutmeg

1 Remove the turkey from its packaging and remove the innards. You can reserve these for gravy. Rinse the turkey under cold water and dry it with a towel.

2 Add all of the ingredients to a pot of water and bring to a boil. Reduce heat and simmer for 20 minutes.

3 Remove from heat and allow the mixture to cool completely.

4 Place the turkey in the brine breast side down. Make sure that the turkey is fully submerged, weighing down with plates if necessary. Refrigerate for 24 hours.

5 Remove the turkey from the brine and dry the bird inside and out. Discard the brine and cook the turkey.

Beer Brine

YIELD: BRINE FOR 10 TO 20 LB. TURKEY
ACTIVE TIME: 45 MINUTES • TOTAL TIME: 24 HOURS

This wet beer brine is a perfect way to subtly infuse hops, barley, and wheat into your turkey. Dark beer adds rich flavor and beautiful color as well.

INGREDIENTS

3 12 oz. bottles of dark beer

½ cup kosher salt

1 cup dark brown sugar

4 bay leaves

3 sprigs thyme

1 onion, peeled and cut into quarters

3 sprigs rosemary

1 tablespoon peppercorns

1 Remove the turkey from its packaging and remove the innards. You can reserve these for gravy. Rinse the turkey under cold water and dry it with a towel.

2 Place turkey and all the ingredients in the brine, adding water if needed so that the turkey is fully submerged.

3 Place the turkey in the brine breast side down. Make sure that the turkey is fully submerged, weighing down with plates if necessary. Refrigerate for 24 hours.

4 Remove the turkey from the brine and dry the bird inside and out. Discard the brine and cook the turkey.

Herb Brine

YIELD: BRINE FOR 10 TO 20 LB. TURKEY
ACTIVE TIME: 10 MINUTES • TOTAL TIME: 24 HOURS

When you want to pack a lot of flavor into your turkey, this is the go-to brine.

1 Remove the turkey from its packaging and remove the innards. You can reserve these for gravy. Rinse the turkey under cold water and dry it with a towel.

2 Combine all ingredients together and mix thoroughly.

3 Rub mixture under the turkey skin, all over the outside, and inside the carcass.

4 Cover the turkey with foil and place in the refrigerator for 24 hours.

INGREDIENTS

¾ cup maple sugar

2 tablespoons salt

2 teaspoons pepper

2 teaspoons lemon zest

2 teaspoons paprika

½ teaspoon cinnamon

½ teaspoon nutmeg

Blood Orange and Bourbon Brine

YIELD: BRINE FOR 10 TO 20 LB. TURKEY
ACTIVE TIME: 10 MINUTES • TOTAL TIME: 24 HOURS

Blood orange and the bourbon's hints of vanilla, oak, and caramel make this unique brine a great way to enhance your next turkey.

INGREDIENTS

3 quarts hot water

¾ cup kosher salt

½ cup brown sugar

5 blood oranges, halved and juiced

2 cinnamon sticks

2 whole star anise

3 whole cloves

3 quarts of ice-cold water

2 cups bourbon (of your preference)

1 In a stockpot combine all the ingredients except the bourbon and cold water. Bring to a full boil and stir to ensure that the salt and sugar dissolve.

2 Remove from the heat, add the bourbon and cold water, and allow to come to room temperature. Once cool, transfer the brine to a container large enough to hold it and the turkey.

3 Remove the turkey from its packaging and remove the innards. You can reserve these for gravy. Rinse the turkey under cold water.

4 Place the turkey in the brine breast side down. Make sure that the turkey is fully submerged, weighing down with plates if necessary. Refrigerate for 24 hours.

Juniper Brine

Dried juniper berries pack a ton of flavor and give your turkey a complex and aromatic taste.

1 In a stockpot combine all the ingredients except the cold water. Bring to a full boil and stir to ensure that the salt and sugar dissolve.

2 Remove from the heat, add the cold water, and allow to come to room temperature. Once cool, transfer the brine to a container large enough to hold it and the turkey.

3 Remove the turkey from its packaging and remove the innards. You can reserve these for gravy. Rinse the turkey under cold water.

4 Place the turkey in the brine breast side down. Make sure that the turkey is fully submerged, weighing down with plates if necessary. Refrigerate for 24 hours.

INGREDIENTS

3 quarts hot water

2/3 cup kosher salt

2/3 cup granulated sugar

2 teaspoons juniper berries, crushed

1 teaspoon white peppercorns, crushed

3 whole cloves

6 garlic cloves, crushed

6 sprigs thyme

2 sprigs rosemary

3 quarts ice-cold water

Earl Grey Tea and Lemon Brine

YIELD: BRINE FOR 10 TO 20 LB. TURKEY
ACTIVE TIME: 10 MINUTES • TOTAL TIME: 24 HOURS

The deep flavor of tea cut by the sweet-and-sour flavor of citrus works incredibly well in this brine.

1 In a stockpot combine all the ingredients except the tea bags and cold water. Bring to a full boil and stir to ensure that the salt and sugar dissolve.

2 Remove from the heat, add the teabags, and allow them to steep for 20 minutes. Remove the tea bags from the pot, add the cold water, and allow to come to room temperature. Once cool, transfer the brine to a container large enough to hold it and the turkey.

3 Remove the turkey from its packaging and remove the innards. You can reserve these for gravy. Rinse the turkey under cold water.

4 Place the turkey in the brine breast side down. Make sure that the turkey is fully submerged, weighing down with plates if necessary. Refrigerate for 24 hours.

INGREDIENTS

3 quarts hot water

¾ cup kosher salt

¾ cup brown sugar

¾ cup honey

3 lemons, halved and juiced

2 oz. fresh ginger, cut in 2 pieces

18 bags Earl Grey tea

3 quarts ice-cold water

White Wine and Garlic Brine

YIELD: BRINE FOR 10 TO 20 LB. TURKEY

ACTIVE TIME: 10 MINUTES • TOTAL TIME: 24 HOURS

This classic combo creates a brine that is sure to impress anyone who happens to grace your dinner table.

INGREDIENTS

3 quarts hot water

¾ cup kosher salt

½ cup granulated sugar

3 lemons, halved and juiced

12 garlic cloves

2 large shallots, peeled and sliced

6 sprigs thyme

1 tablespoon whole coriander

2 teaspoons white peppercorns

3 cups dry white wine (about 750ml bottle)

3 quarts ice-cold water

1 In a stockpot combine all the ingredients except the white wine and cold water. Bring to a full boil and stir to ensure that the salt and sugar dissolves.

2 Remove from the heat, add the wine and cold water, and allow to come to room temperature. Once cool, transfer the brine to a container large enough to hold both it and the turkey.

3 Remove the turkey from its packaging and remove the innards. You can reserve these for gravy. Rinse the turkey under cold water.

4 Place the turkey in the brine breast side down. Make sure that the turkey is fully submerged, weighing down with plates if necessary. Refrigerate for 24 hours.

Cajun Dry Brine

YIELD: BRINE FOR 10 TO 20 LB. TURKEY
ACTIVE TIME: 10 MINUTES • TOTAL TIME: 24 HOURS

Vibrant, smoky, and complex, this brine is a great way to put a new spin on your turkey dinner. Make sure to have leftover turkey with this brine, because the sandwiches are second to none!

INGREDIENTS

⅓ cup kosher salt

¼ cup brown sugar

½ cup smoked paprika

¼ cup chili powder

2 teaspoons garlic powder

2 teaspoons onion powder

¼ teaspoon cayenne pepper

2 teaspoons mustard powder

1 tablespoon black pepper

1 Remove the turkey from its packaging and take out the innards. You can reserve these for gravy. Rinse the turkey under cold water and dry it with a towel.

2 Combine all ingredients together and mix thoroughly.

3 Rub mixture under the turkey skin, all over the outside, and inside the carcass.

4 Cover the turkey with foil and place in the refrigerator for 24 hours.

Citrus and Peppercorn Dry Brine

YIELD: BRINE FOR 10 TO 20 LB. TURKEY
ACTIVE TIME: 10 MINUTES • TOTAL TIME: 24 HOURS

The pop of citrus coupled with the spicy peppercorns will elevate your bird to a whole new level.

1 Remove the turkey from its packaging and take out the innards. You can reserve these for gravy. Rinse the turkey under cold water and dry it with a towel.

2 Crack the peppercorns using a spice grinder or a mortar and pestle. Then, combine all ingredients together and mix thoroughly.

3 Rub mixture under the turkey skin, all over the outside, and inside the carcass.

4 Cover the turkey with foil and place in the refrigerator for 24 hours.

INGREDIENTS

2 teaspoons black peppercorns

2 teaspoons pink peppercorns

2 teaspoons green peppercorns

⅓ cup kosher salt

¼ cup brown sugar

2 teaspoons mustard powder

3 tablespoons lemon zest

6 tablespoon orange zest

2 teaspoons dried parsley

2 teaspoons dried thyme

Fennel, Lime, and Chili Dry Brine

YIELD: BRINE FOR 10 TO 20 LB. TURKEY
ACTIVE TIME: 10 MINUTES • TOTAL TIME: 24 HOURS

Fennel, lime, and chili powder give this brine a spicy yet bright flavor.

INGREDIENTS

1 tablespoon black peppercorns

1/3 cup kosher salt

1/4 cup granulated sugar

1/4 cup chili powder

2 teaspoons garlic powder

2 tablespoons fennel seeds

1 tablespoon coriander seeds

3 tablespoons lime zest

1 Remove the turkey from its packaging and take out the innards. You can reserve these for gravy. Rinse the turkey under cold water and dry it with a towel.

2 Crack the peppercorns, fennel, and coriander in a spice grinder or mortar and pestle and then combine all ingredients together and mix thoroughly.

3 Rub mixture under the turkey skin, all over the outside, and inside the carcass.

4 Cover the turkey with foil and place in the refrigerator for 24 hours.

Orange and Thyme Dry Brine

YIELD: BRINE FOR 10 TO 20 LB. TURKEY
ACTIVE TIME: 10 MINUTES • TOTAL TIME: 24 HOURS

These two complementary flavors yield wonderful results.

1 Remove the turkey from its packaging and take out the innards. You can reserve these for gravy. Rinse the turkey under cold water and dry it with a towel.

2 Crack the peppercorns using a spice grinder or mortar and pestle. Then, combine all ingredients together and mix thoroughly.

3 Rub mixture under the turkey skin, all over the outside, and inside the carcass.

4 Cover the turkey with foil and place in the refrigerator for 24 hours.

INGREDIENTS

1 teaspoon black peppercorns

⅓ cup kosher salt

¼ cup brown sugar

5 tablespoons orange zest

1 tablespoon dried thyme

Sage and Garlic Dry Brine

YIELD: BRINE FOR 10 TO 20 LB. TURKEY
ACTIVE TIME: 10 MINUTES • TOTAL TIME: 24 HOURS

There is a tendency to oversaturate turkey in a brine with lots of ingredients. But the simplicity of sage and garlic provides a mouthwatering turkey.

1 Remove the turkey from its packaging and take out the innards. You can reserve these for gravy. Rinse the turkey under cold water and dry it with a towel.

2 Crack the peppercorns using a spice grinder or mortar and pestle. Then, combine all ingredients together and mix thoroughly.

3 Rub mixture under the turkey skin, all over the outside, and inside the carcass.

4 Cover the turkey with foil and place in the refrigerator for 24 hours.

INGREDIENTS

1 teaspoon black peppercorns

⅓ cup kosher salt

⅛ cup granulated sugar

¼ cup fresh sage, chopped

6 garlic cloves, chopped

2 teaspoons dried parsley

Lemon and Rosemary Dry Brine

YIELD: BRINE FOR 10 TO 20 LB. TURKEY
ACTIVE TIME: 10 MINUTES • TOTAL TIME: 24 HOURS

When you add the sharp, piney flavor of rosemary and the sweet, tart burst of lemon to turkey, the results are astounding.

INGREDIENTS

2 teaspoons white peppercorns

⅓ cup kosher salt

⅛ cup granulated sugar

2 teaspoons garlic, chopped

¼ cup lemon zest

2 tablespoons fresh rosemary, chopped

2 teaspoons fresh thyme, chopped

1 Remove the turkey from its packaging and take out the innards. You can reserve these for gravy. Rinse the turkey under cold water and dry it with a towel.

2 Crack the peppercorns using a spice grinder or mortar and pestle. Then, combine all ingredients together and mix thoroughly.

3 Rub mixture under the turkey skin, all over the outside, and inside the carcass.

4 Cover the turkey with foil and place in the refrigerator for 24 hours.

Rubs

Three-Pepper Rub

YIELD: RUB FOR 10 TO 20 LB. TURKEY
ACTIVE TIME: 10 MINUTES • TOTAL TIME: 10 MINUTES

Smoky, spicy, and so good, this is a great way to add a bit of kick to a turkey.

INGREDIENTS

1 tablespoon black peppercorns

⅓ cup kosher salt

2 teaspoons mustard powder

1 tablespoon smoked paprika

2 teaspoons chili flakes

2 teaspoons dried parsley

2 teaspoons dried thyme

2 teaspoons garlic powder

1 Remove the turkey from its packaging and take out the innards. You can reserve these for gravy. Rinse the turkey under cold water and dry with a towel.

2 Crack the peppercorns using a spice grinder or mortar and pestle. Then, combine all ingredients together and mix thoroughly.

3 Rub mixture under the turkey skin, all over the outside, and inside of the carcass.

Herb Rub

The sweet notes of the basil and lavender combine for an aromatic rub perfect for oven-roasted turkey.

1 Remove the turkey from its packaging and take out the innards. You can reserve these for gravy. Rinse the turkey under cold water and dry with a towel.

2 Remove the herbs from their stems and chop. Put off to the side. Grind the fennel, coriander, and bay leaves using a spice grinder or mortar and pestle. Then, combine all ingredients together and mix thoroughly.

3 Rub mixture under the turkey skin, all over the outside, and inside of the carcass.

INGREDIENTS

¼ cup parsley

2 tablespoons rosemary

2 tablespoons thyme

2 tablespoons basil

1 tablespoon oregano

1 tablespoon sage

2 tablespoons dried lavender

1 tablespoon white pepper

1 tablespoon fennel seeds

1 tablespoon coriander seeds

2 bay leaves

⅓ cup kosher salt

Smoked Lemon Zest Rub

YIELD: RUB FOR 10 TO 20 LB. TURKEY
ACTIVE TIME: 25 MINUTES • TOTAL TIME: 25 MINUTES

Peppercorns and lemon zest bring out some of a turkey's natural sweetness. This rub works well for a variety of different cooking methods.

INGREDIENTS

¼ cup lemon zest

2 tablespoons assorted peppercorns

1 tablespoon coriander

⅓ cup kosher salt

2 teaspoons granulated sugar

¼ cup parsley, chopped

2 tablespoons garlic, chopped

1 tablespoon oregano, chopped

1 Remove the turkey from its packaging and take out the innards. You can reserve these for gravy. Rinse the turkey under cold water and dry it with a towel.

2 Fill a smoking gun with your preferred wood chips. Place lemon zest in a bowl and line the top with plastic wrap, leaving only a small opening for the hose of the smoking gun. Insert the tip of the hose and light the wood chips. Then, turn the machine on. Allow smoke to sit with the lemon zest for 10 minutes. Repeat the process until the desired level of smokiness is achieved.

3 Grind the peppercorns and coriander using a spice grinder or mortar and pestle. Then, combine all ingredients together and mix thoroughly.

4 Rub mixture under the turkey skin, all over the outside, and inside the carcass.

Spicy Rub

YIELD: RUB FOR 10 TO 20 LB. TURKEY
ACTIVE TIME: 10 MINUTES • TOTAL TIME: 10 MINUTES

This turkey rub brings some serious spice with the addition of cayenne, paprika, and Dijon. This is a perfect rub to use when smoking a turkey.

INGREDIENTS

- ⅓ cup kosher salt
- 2 tablespoons black pepper
- 1 tablespoon sweet paprika
- 1 tablespoon cayenne pepper
- 1 tablespoon chili flakes
- 2 tablespoons garlic, chopped
- 1 tablespoon ginger, chopped
- 1 tablespoon hot sauce
- 1 tablespoon Dijon mustard

1 Remove the turkey from its packaging and take out the innards. You can reserve these for gravy. Rinse the turkey under cold water and dry it with a towel.

2 Combine all the dry spices and set aside. In a bowl, mix together the ginger, garlic, hot sauce, and mustard. Combine the wet and dry ingredients.

3 Rub mixture under the turkey skin, all over the outside, and inside the carcass.

Brown Sugar and Ancho Chili Rub

YIELD: RUB FOR 10 TO 20 LB. TURKEY
ACTIVE TIME: 10 MINUTES • TOTAL TIME: 10 MINUTES

This brown sugar and ancho rub works well for many techniques, so you'll always be able to keep up with demand.

1 Remove the turkey from its packaging and take out the innards. You can reserve these for gravy. Rinse the turkey under cold water and dry it with a towel.

2 Combine all ingredients together in a bowl and mix thoroughly.

3 Rub mixture under the turkey skin, all over the outside, and inside the carcass.

INGREDIENTS

⅓ cup kosher salt

½ cup brown sugar

½ cup ancho chili powder

1 tablespoon black pepper

2 tablespoons garlic powder

2 tablespoons onion powder

1 tablespoon mustard powder

2 tablespoons coriander

2 tablespoons cinnamon

Jerk Spice Rub

YIELD: RUB FOR 10 TO 20 LB. TURKEY
ACTIVE TIME: 15 MINUTES • TOTAL TIME: 15 MINUTES

The deep flavor of the habaneros cut by the sharp tang of the cinnamon makes this rub second to none.

1 Remove the turkey from its packaging and take out the innards. You can reserve these for gravy. Rinse the turkey under cold water and dry it with a towel.

2 Combine the dry spices, sugar, and salt and set aside. Mix together the garlic, ginger, habaneros, lime, olive oil, thyme, and scallions. Combine all ingredients and mix together.

3 Rub mixture under the turkey skin, all over the outside, and inside the carcass.

INGREDIENTS

2 tablespoons black pepper

2 teaspoons cinnamon

½ teaspoon nutmeg

½ teaspoon ground cloves

⅓ cup kosher salt

¼ cup brown sugar

2 tablespoons garlic, chopped

1 tablespoon ginger, chopped

2 habaneros, stemmed and chopped (may remove seeds to reduce the spice)

¼ cup fresh lime juice

½ cup olive oil

1 tablespoon thyme, chopped

2 tablespoons scallions, sliced

Holiday Rub

YIELD: RUB FOR 10 TO 20 LB. TURKEY
ACTIVE TIME: 10 MINUTES • TOTAL TIME: 10 MINUTES

The allspice and ginger will give your bird a wonderful taste that your whole family will love.

INGREDIENTS

- ⅓ cup kosher salt
- ¼ cup brown sugar
- 1 tablespoon black pepper
- 1 tablespoon allspice
- 1 tablespoon ginger powder
- 1 tablespoon dried sage
- 1 tablespoon dried thyme
- 2 tablespoons orange zest

1 Remove the turkey from its packaging and take out the innards. You can reserve these for gravy. Rinse the turkey under cold water and dry it with a towel.

2 Combine all ingredients together in a bowl and mix thoroughly.

3 Rub mixture under the turkey skin, all over the outside, and inside the carcass.

BBQ Rub

YIELD: RUB FOR 10 TO 20 LB. TURKEY
ACTIVE TIME: 15 MINUTES • TOTAL TIME: 15 MINUTES

The smokiness of the paprika and the heat of the chili powder bring out the turkey's natural juices.

1 Remove the turkey from its packaging and take out the innards. You can reserve these for gravy. Rinse the turkey under cold water and dry it with a towel.

2 Combine all ingredients together in a bowl and mix thoroughly.

3 Rub mixture under the turkey skin, all over the outside, and inside the carcass.

INGREDIENTS

⅓ cup kosher salt

½ cup brown sugar

¼ cup smoked paprika

1 tablespoon cayenne pepper

1 tablespoon chili powder

2 teaspoons cumin

1 tablespoon onion powder

2 tablespoons garlic powder

1 tablespoon black pepper

1 tablespoon fennel seeds

1 tablespoon coriander

1 tablespoon mustard powder

Gravy

Traditional Gravy

YIELD: ABOUT 6 CUPS • ACTIVE TIME: 30 MINUTES • TOTAL TIME: 30 MINUTES

The sweetness of the white wine and shallots give this gravy an unexpected punch.

1 After turkey is roasted, transfer to a resting rack. Pour the pan drippings into a large, heat-resistant measuring cup. Allow time for the fat to settle on the surface. Placing the drippings in the fridge or freezer will help speed up the process. Skim off the fat and reserve.

2 Place your roasting pan over medium-high heat. Add the butter and turkey fat to the pan. Once hot, add the shallots and garlic and cook until translucent. Stir constantly to prevent sticking. Next, add your fresh herbs and toast in the pan for 20 seconds.

3 Deglaze with the white wine and allow the liquid to evaporate.

4 Add the flour to the pan and cook for a few minutes while stirring to prevent burning. The consistency should be that of wet sand. Continue to cook until you smell a nutty aroma.

5 Add the pan drippings slowly and whisk thoroughly to ensure you do not have lumps. The mixture should look like a paste.

6 Add 1 cup of the stock, whisking slowly while you pour. Slowly stir in the remainder of the stock. You can add more stock for a thinner gravy, or let the liquid reduce for a thicker gravy.

7 Season to taste with salt and pepper.

INGREDIENTS

½ cup turkey fat skimmed from drippings

¼ cup butter

2 cups pan drippings with the fat skimmed off and reserved to make the roux

¼ cup shallots or Spanish onions, chopped

2 tablespoons garlic, chopped

2 tablespoons thyme, chopped

1 tablespoon sage, chopped

2 teaspoons rosemary, chopped

¼ cup white wine

¼ cup flour, sifted

4 cups turkey or chicken stock

Salt and black pepper, to taste

Giblet Gravy

YIELD: ABOUT 5 CUPS • ACTIVE TIME: 1 HOUR AND 30 MINUTES
TOTAL TIME: 1 HOUR AND 30 MINUTES

Cooking with the innards of the turkey may seem daunting, but it utilizes the whole bird and yields the best gravy.

1 In a saucepot heat the vegetable oil. Then, add the giblets and sear until browned on all sides.

2 In the same pan, add the onions, garlic, celery, and carrot. Stir every couple of minutes until fully browned.

3 Cover with water and add the thyme and rosemary sprigs. Bring to a boil. Then, drop to a low simmer. Allow this stock to cook for about an hour for the flavors to develop. You should be left with about 4 cups of stock.

4 Once the time has passed, strain the stock and set aside. Discard all but the turkey neck from the strainer, then transfer the neck to a cutting board. Do your best to remove the meat from the neck and reserve. Discard the bones.

5 Place the saucepot back on the stove top and melt the butter.

6 Add the flour to the pan and cook for a few minutes while stirring to prevent burning. The consistency should be that of wet sand. Cook until you smell a nutty aroma.

7 Add 1 cup of the stock slowly, whisking while you pour. You will have a paste. Slowly stream in the remainder of the stock. You can add more stock for a thinner gravy or let the liquid reduce for a thicker gravy.

8 Add the neck meat to the gravy and cook until warmed through.

9 Taste and season with the salt and pepper.

INGREDIENTS

2 tablespoons vegetable oil

Turkey innards: neck, heart, liver, and gizzard

1 cup shallots or Spanish onions, sliced

½ cup celery

½ cup carrot

4 garlic cloves, sliced

5 cups water

3 sprigs thyme

1 sprig rosemary

½ cup butter

½ cup flour, sifted

1 cup turkey stock (see page 86)

Salt and black pepper, to taste

Vegetarian Gravy

YIELD: ABOUT 5 CUPS • ACTIVE TIME: 30 MINUTES • TOTAL TIME: 30 MINUTES

This gravy proves that vegetarian doesn't mean bland. Even the most fervent meat lover will come away impressed.

1 Melt the butter in a saucepan. Once melted, add all of the vegetables and cook until browned. Next, add your fresh herbs and toast in the pan for 20 seconds until all the vegetables are coated.

2 Deglaze with the sherry and allow the liquid to evaporate.

3 Add the flour to the pan and cook for a few minutes while stirring to prevent burning. The consistency should be that of wet sand. Cook until you smell a nutty aroma.

4 Add 1 cup of the stock slowly, whisking while you pour. The mixture should resemble a paste. Slowly whisk in the remainder of the stock. You can add more stock for a thinner gravy or let the liquid reduce for a thicker gravy.

5 Taste the gravy and season with salt and pepper.

INGREDIENTS

¼ cup butter

½ cup carrots, chopped

½ cup celery, chopped

¼ cup mushrooms, chopped

1 cup onion, chopped

2 tablespoons garlic, chopped

2 tablespoons thyme, chopped

1 tablespoon sage, chopped

2 teaspoons rosemary, chopped

½ cup sherry

¼ cup flour, sifted

4 cups vegetable stock

Salt and black pepper, to taste

Turkey Stock

Turkey stock is a key component of a good turkey gravy, especially if you deep fry or smoke your bird and don't have pan drippings at your disposal.

INGREDIENTS

1 turkey carcass

2 tablespoons peppercorns

1 medium onion, quartered (also feel free to use onion scraps)

2 carrots, cut into 1-inch pieces

2 celery stalks, cut into 1-inch pieces

5 sprigs parsley

3 bay leaves

1 Combine all ingredients along with enough cold water to cover the turkey carcass, about 5 quarts. Bring to a boil, then reduce the heat so that it simmers.

2 Skim the surface of the stock to get rid of any fat and impurities.

3 Continue to simmer until the stock reduces by at least a third.

4 Strain the stock through a mesh strainer and discard any solids. This stock can be kept in the refrigerator for up to 2 weeks or in the freezer for 3 months.

Traditional Cranberry Sauce

Once you try this homemade version, you'll never go back to canned.

INGREDIENTS

12 oz. fresh cranberries

1 cup sugar

1 tablespoon water

1 Add three-quarters of the cranberries to a pot along with the sugar and water. Cook on medium heat until the cranberries start to burst.

2 Lower the heat to medium-low, stir in the remaining cranberries, and cook until desired thickness is achieved.

3 Remove from heat and chill in the refrigerator until ready to serve.

Orange and Jalapeño Cranberry Sauce

SERVINGS: 4 TO 6 • ACTIVE TIME: 5 MINUTES • TOTAL TIME: 20 MINUTES

The jalapeños and orange zest transport this traditional side into the 21st century.

1 Add three-quarters of the cranberries to a pot along with the sugar, orange juice, orange zest, and jalapeño. Cook over on medium heat until the cranberries start to burst.

2 Lower the heat to medium-low, stir in the remaining cranberries, and cook until desired thickness is achieved.

3 Remove from heat and chill in the refrigerator until ready to serve.

INGREDIENTS

12 oz. fresh cranberries

1 cup sugar

¼ cup orange juice

1 strip of orange zest

1 jalapeño, diced

NOTE: To put a smoky spin on this recipe, roast the jalapeños first in the oven at 400°F until golden brown and soft. Then, place in a blender with the orange juice and add to the cranberry sauce as directed.

Stuffing

Traditional Stuffing

SERVINGS: 6 TO 8 • ACTIVE TIME: 15 MINUTES • TOTAL TIME: 1 HOUR

Once you make this recipe, you'll never buy boxed stuffing again.

INGREDIENTS

1 Preheat oven to 350°F.

2 Grease a 3-quart baking dish and add the dried bread.

3 In a large pan, melt the butter. Add the onion and celery, and cook until soft, about 5 minutes.

4 Add the stock along with the salt, pepper, sage, thyme, and rosemary. Bring to a boil, then reduce heat to a simmer for 10 minutes.

5 Pour the stock mixture over the bread in the baking dish. Cover the dish and bake for 30 minutes.

6 Uncover the dish and bake for an additional 25 to 30 minutes, until the top of the mixture begins to brown.

13 cups bread, cubed and dried

1 cup unsalted butter

1 medium onion, diced

4 celery stalks, chopped

1 cup turkey stock (see page 86)

1 tablespoon salt

1 teaspoon pepper

1 tablespoon dried sage

2 teaspoons dried thyme

2 teaspoons dried rosemary

Bacon, Pear, and Rosemary Stuffing

SERVINGS: 6 TO 8 • ACTIVE TIME: 15 MINUTES
TOTAL TIME: 1 HOUR AND 30 MINUTES

With the addition of smoky bacon, sweet pears, and fragrant rosemary, this stuffing won't stay on the table for long.

1 Preheat oven to 350°F.

2 Grease a 3-quart baking dish and spread the bread evenly in the dish.

3 In a large pan, cook the bacon over medium heat until brown.

4 With a slotted spoon, scoop out the bacon and drain on a paper towel.

5 Keep the bacon grease in the pan. Add onion and celery and cook until soft, about 5 minutes.

6 Add the stock to the pan along with the salt, pepper, sage, pears, and rosemary. Bring to a boil, then reduce heat to a simmer for 10 minutes.

7 Pour the stock mixture over the bread in the baking dish.

8 Cover the dish and bake for 30 minutes.

9 Uncover the dish and bake for an additional 25 to 30 minutes, until the top of the mixture begins to brown.

INGREDIENTS

13 cups bread,
cubed and dried

1 lb. bacon

1 medium onion, diced

4 celery stalks, chopped

1 cup turkey stock
(see page 86)

1 tablespoon salt

1 teaspoon pepper

1 tablespoon dried sage

4 pears, peeled, cored,
and cut into slices

3 sprigs rosemary

Challah, Sautéed Onion, and Goat Cheese Stuffing

SERVINGS: 6 TO 8 • ACTIVE TIME: 15 MINUTES • TOTAL TIME: 1 HOUR

The challah bread adds a rich, buttery flavor that is sure to please.

INGREDIENTS

13 cups challah bread, cubed and dried

3 tablespoons unsalted butter

2 medium onions, sliced

4 celery stalks, chopped

1 cup turkey stock (see page 86)

1 tablespoon salt

1 teaspoon pepper

1 tablespoon dried sage

2 tablespoons fresh thyme

8 oz. goat cheese

1 Preheat oven to 350°F. Grease a 3-quart baking dish and place the bread into the dish.

2 In a large pan over medium heat, melt the butter. Add the onions and celery and cook until they start to brown, about 10 minutes.

3 Add the stock to the pan along with the salt, pepper, sage, and thyme. Bring to a boil, then reduce heat to a simmer for 10 minutes.

4 Pour the stock mixture over the bread in the baking dish.

5 Crumble the goat cheese and mix it into the stuffing. Cover the dish and bake for 30 minutes.

6 Uncover the dish and bake for an additional 25 to 30 minutes, until the top of the mixture begins to brown.

Mushroom and Cornbread Stuffing

SERVINGS: 6 TO 8 • ACTIVE TIME: 15 MINUTES • TOTAL TIME: 1 HOUR

While not the traditional go-to for stuffing, this combination of cornbread and mushrooms makes for a savory side.

1 Prepare the cornbread. Cool, then crumble into a greased 3-quart baking dish.

2 Preheat oven to 350°F.

3 In a large pan, melt the butter over medium heat. Then, add the onion, celery, and mushrooms and cook until they start to brown, about 10 minutes.

4 Add the stock to the pan along with the salt, pepper, sage, and rosemary. Bring to a boil, then reduce heat to simmer for 10 minutes.

5 Pour the stock mixture over the bread in the baking dish. Bake uncovered for 30 minutes.

INGREDIENTS

Cornbread
(see page 233)

3 tablespoons butter

1 medium onion, sliced

2 celery stalks, chopped

6 oz. mushrooms

1 cup turkey stock
(see page 86)

1 tablespoon salt

1 teaspoon pepper

1 tablespoon dried sage

2 sprigs rosemary

INGREDIENTS

13 cups of bread, cubed and dried

1 lb. sausage (casings removed)

1 medium onion, sliced

2 celery stalks, chopped

1 cup turkey stock (see page 86)

1 tablespoon salt

1 teaspoon pepper

1 tablespoon dried sage

4 apples (Granny Smith or Cortland), peeled, cored, and diced

6 oz. pecans, crushed

Sausage, Apple, and Pecan Stuffing

SERVINGS: 6 TO 8 • ACTIVE TIME: 15 MINUTES
TOTAL TIME: 1 HOUR AND 30 MINUTES

The deep flavor of pecans perfectly complements the sweet apples and smoky sausage.

1 Preheat oven to 350°F. Grease a 3-quart baking dish and place the bread into it.

2 Brown the sausage in a large pan over medium heat, pressing down on the links with a wooden spoon to break them up. Remove the sausage with a slotted spoon and set aside.

3 Cook the onion and celery in the sausage grease until they start to brown, about 10 minutes.

4 Add the stock to the pan along with the salt, pepper, sage, and browned sausage. Bring to a boil, then reduce heat to a simmer for 10 minutes.

5 Pour the stock mixture over the bread in the baking dish.

6 Add the apples to the stuffing mixture and mix everything together.

7 Add the pecans to the top of the stuffing. Cover the dish and bake for 30 minutes.

8 Uncover the dish and bake for an additional 25 to 30 minutes until the top of the mixture begins to brown.

Savory Sausage Stuffing

**SERVINGS: 8 TO 10 • ACTIVE TIME: 20 MINUTES
TOTAL TIME: 50 MINUTES**

Even if you choose to stuff your bird, it's great to have an extra dish of stuffing. Using the slow cooker to prepare it frees up room in your oven and keeps the stuffing moist.

1 Preheat oven to 350°F. Cut sausages into bite-sized pieces. In a large skillet, cook sausage over medium-high heat until browned and cooked through. Transfer cooked meat to a large bowl with a slotted spoon.

2 Pour all but ¼ cup of the fat from skillet. Add the apples, onion, and celery and cook, while stirring, until onion is translucent, about 5 minutes. Add the onion mixture to the bowl with the sausage.

3 Stir the bread into the bowl. Add thyme, salt, and pepper, and stir to combine. Put mixture into a greased baking dish.

4 In a bowl, whisk the eggs together and add the chicken stock or broth. Pour over bread mixture. Dot with the butter pieces.

5 Bake uncovered for 30 minutes. Transfer to a serving bowl and garnish with the chopped parsley.

INGREDIENTS

1 lb. Italian sausage, sweet, spicy, or a combination

3 large apples, peeled and cored

1 large onion, diced

1 cup celery, diced

6 cups bread crumbs or 10 cups bread, dried and cubed

1 teaspoon fresh thyme, chopped

1 teaspoon salt, plus more to taste

½ teaspoon pepper, plus more to taste

3 eggs

6 cups chicken stock or broth

1 cup butter, cut into pieces

¼ cup fresh parsley, chopped, for garnish

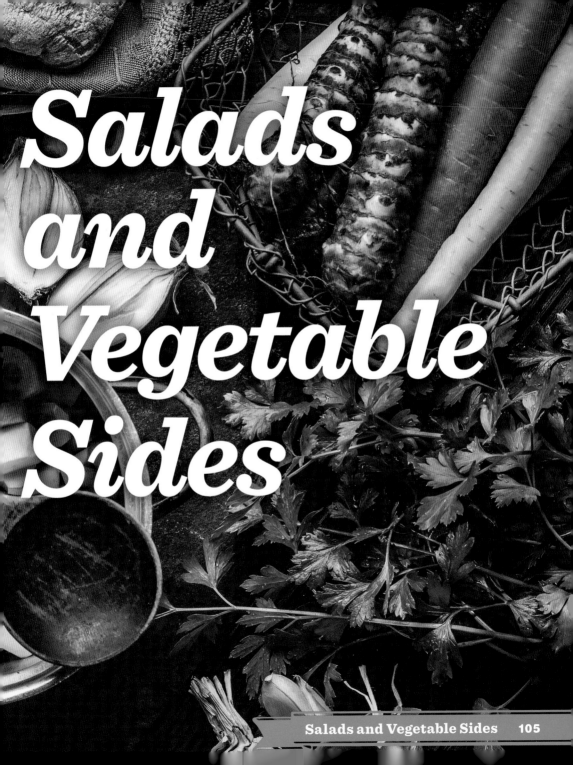

Salads and Vegetable Sides

Caesar Salad

Don't turn your nose up at the anchovy fillets; they're essential to this classic.

INGREDIENTS

3 heads of romaine lettuce

2 garlic cloves, minced

½ small lemon, juiced

1 large egg

4 anchovy fillets

1 teaspoon Dijon mustard

½ cup olive oil

Sea salt and coarsely ground black pepper, to taste

Croutons (optional)

1 Rinse the heads of romaine lettuce and dry thoroughly. Place in refrigerator.

2 In a small bowl, whisk the garlic, lemon juice, and egg together until blended. Whisk in the anchovy fillets and Dijon mustard until the anchovies are completely incorporated into the dressing.

3 Gradually whisk in the olive oil and season with coarsely ground black pepper and sea salt. Place the dressing in the refrigerator for about 15 minutes. Pour over the chilled lettuce. If using, add croutons before serving.

INGREDIENTS

⅓ lb. arugula,
rinsed and stemmed

6 medium red beets,
peeled

¼ cup olive oil,
plus 2 tablespoons

¼ cup sunflower seeds

2 tablespoons
balsamic vinegar

Sea salt and coarsely
ground black pepper,
to taste

Grilled Beets and Toasted Sunflower Seeds over Arugula

SERVINGS: 6 • ACTIVE TIME: 15 MINUTES • TOTAL TIME: 20 MINUTES

The brightness of the beets combined with the mellow undertones of the sunflower seeds give this simple salad an incredible taste.

1 Rinse the arugula and then dry thoroughly. Place in the refrigerator to chill.

2 Cut the beets into quarters and combine with olive oil in a small bowl. Let stand for 30 minutes.

3 Place a medium cast-iron skillet on your gas or charcoal grill and warm it to medium-high heat. Leave the grill covered while heating, as this will add a faint, smoky flavor to the skillet.

4 Once the grill reaches between 400°F and 500°F, transfer the beets onto the grill. Grill the beets until tender, about 10 minutes. Transfer the beets to a large bowl and cover with aluminum foil.

5 Add the sunflower seeds into the cast-iron skillet and cook until browned, about 2 minutes. Remove and mix with the beets. Set aside.

6 In a small bowl, add the remaining olive oil and the balsamic vinegar and mix thoroughly. Drizzle on top of beets and sunflower seeds, and place over chilled arugula. Season with salt and pepper before serving.

Spinach Salad with Bacon and Eggs

The sweetness of the onion and the crispiness of the bacon in this salad pair well with smoked turkey.

1 Place the bacon in a cast-iron skillet and cook over medium heat until crispy. Remove from the skillet and set on paper towels to drain. Crumble when cool.

2 Rinse the spinach and dry thoroughly. Place in a medium bowl and store in the refrigerator.

3 Fill a medium saucepan with water and place over medium heat. Bring to a boil, add the eggs, and remove from heat. Cover the saucepan and let the eggs rest in the hot water for about 10 to 14 minutes. Remove from water and let cool in the refrigerator.

4 In a small bowl, whisk together the vinegars, Dijon mustard, and olive oil and set aside.

5 Remove the eggs from the refrigerator and peel off the shells. Slice the eggs in half and add to the spinach. Drizzle the dressing onto the spinach. Top with the bacon bits and sliced onion. Season with salt and pepper and serve.

INGREDIENTS

8 thick slices of bacon, trimmed of excess fat

1 lb. spinach

3 large eggs

2 tablespoons white wine vinegar

2 tablespoons red wine vinegar

1 teaspoon Dijon mustard

2 tablespoons olive oil

1 medium red onion, sliced

Sea salt and coarsely ground black pepper

INGREDIENTS

8 thick slices of maple-smoked bacon, trimmed of excess fat

1 pound spinach, stemmed

1 medium red onion, sliced into ¼-inch rings

¼ cup dried cranberries

2 tablespoons balsamic vinegar

1 teaspoon Dijon mustard

1 teaspoon red pepper flakes (optional)

½ cup olive oil

Sea salt and coarsely ground black pepper, to taste

Sunflower seeds, for garnish

NOTE:
For additional heat, feel free to add a couple peperoncini.

Spinach Salad with Maple-Smoked Bacon

SERVINGS: 6 • ACTIVE TIME: 35 MINUTES • TOTAL TIME: 45 MINUTES

The hint of smoke from the bacon and the tartness of cranberries make this salad a must-have once the weather turns cool.

1 Place the bacon in a cast-iron skillet and cook over medium heat until crispy. Remove from the skillet and set on paper towels to drain. Crumble when cool enough to handle.

2 Rinse the stemmed spinach and dry thoroughly. Place the spinach in a medium bowl and mix in the red onion and dried cranberries. Transfer to the refrigerator.

3 In a small bowl, whisk together the balsamic vinegar, Dijon mustard, and red pepper flakes, if using. Then gradually incorporate the olive oil. Season with salt and pepper and mix into the spinach salad. Add the bacon bits, garnish with sunflower seeds, and serve.

Broccoli Salad

The bacon and cheddar make this salad incredibly filling, so make sure to pair it with lighter sides.

INGREDIENTS

1 head of broccoli

6 to 8 slices of bacon, cooked and crumbled

½ cup red onion, minced

½ cup raisins

8 oz. sharp cheddar, cut into small cubes or grated

1 cup mayonnaise

2 tablespoons white vinegar

¼ cup sugar

Salt and pepper, to taste

1 Cut the broccoli into bite-sized pieces and place into a large bowl.

2 Add the crumbled bacon, onion, raisins, and cheese.

3 In a separate small bowl, mix together the remaining ingredients for the dressing. Add the dressing to the broccoli mixture and toss gently to evenly coat. Salt to taste and serve.

Arugula Salad with Tarragon-Shallot Vinaigrette

The tarragon ensures that this salad doesn't taste anywhere near as light as it actually is.

1 Rinse the arugula and then dry thoroughly. Place in the refrigerator.

2 In a small bowl, whisk together the shallot, tarragon, lemon juice, and Dijon mustard. Then slowly add in the olive oil and red wine vinegar.

3 Season with the salt and pepper and pour over the arugula. Serve immediately.

INGREDIENTS

1 lb. arugula, stemmed

1 shallot, minced

5 sprigs tarragon, minced

¼ small lemon, juiced

1 teaspoon Dijon mustard

½ cup extra virgin olive oil

3 tablespoons red wine vinegar

Sea salt and black pepper, to taste

House Salad

A kitchen-honored classic, the balanced taste of this salad pairs well with the more savory sides in this book.

INGREDIENTS

3 heads of romaine lettuce

1 small red onion, sliced into ¼-inch rings

10 Kalamata olives

10 green olives

4 plum tomatoes, stemmed and quartered

6 peperoncini

2 garlic cloves, minced

¼ cup red wine vinegar

¾ cup extra virgin olive oil

Sea salt and black pepper, to taste

1 Rinse the heads of lettuce and dry them thoroughly. Chop and place in a medium bowl. Combine the lettuce, red onion, Kalamata olives, green olives, tomatoes, and peperoncini. Set in the refrigerator.

2 In a small jar, whisk together the garlic, red wine vinegar, and olive oil. Then, season with the coarsely sea salt and pepper. Chill in the refrigerator for 15 minutes.

3 Remove the salad and vinaigrette from the refrigerator. Mix together immediately before serving.

Chickpea and Carrot Salad

SERVINGS: 6 • ACTIVE TIME: 15 MINUTES • TOTAL TIME: 45 MINUTES

The nutty chickpeas and sweet carrots will match well with any preparation of turkey.

1 Combine chickpeas, carrots, celery, green onions, dill, and toasted pumpkin seeds in a medium bowl and set aside.

2 To make the dressing, combine the olive oil, vinegar, garlic, salt, and pepper. Whisk together until well combined and pour over the salad mixture. Stir well to combine.

3 Allow the salad to chill in the refrigerator for 30 minutes before serving.

INGREDIENTS

- 2 (15 oz.) cans of chickpeas, rinsed and drained, or 3 cups cooked chickpeas
- 2 cups carrots (about 5 to 6 medium carrots), chopped
- ⅔ cup celery, chopped
- ½ cup thinly sliced green onions
- ½ cup dill, chopped
- ½ cup pumpkin seeds, toasted
- ⅓ cup extra virgin olive oil
- 2 to 3 tablespoons sherry vinegar
- 1 medium to large garlic clove, pressed or minced
- ¼ teaspoon salt
- Coarsely ground black pepper, to taste

Roasted Brussels Sprouts with Cranberry and Walnut Honey

SERVINGS: 6 TO 8 • ACTIVE TIME: 15 MINUTES
TOTAL TIME: 45 MINUTES TO 1 HOUR

This recipe will convert even the most diehard Brussels sprouts hater into a fan. Coupling the nutty flavor of roasted Brussels sprouts with cranberry and walnut honey makes a side dish that is unforgettable.

INGREDIENTS

3 lbs. fresh Brussels sprouts

2 tablespoons olive oil

Pinch of salt

6 oz. honey

3 tablespoons cranberry sauce or dried cranberries

4 oz. walnuts, crumbled

1 teaspoon pepper

1 Preheat oven to 425°F.

2 Wash and cut the Brussels sprouts in half length-wise.

3 Toss the cut sprouts in a bowl with olive oil and salt. Place the sprouts on a baking sheet and cook for 25 to 35 minutes, or until brown.

4 While the sprouts are baking, combine the honey and the cranberry component and mix well.

5 Toss the finished sprouts in a bowl along with the honey mixture and half of the walnuts.

6 Season with pepper and top with the remaining walnuts.

INGREDIENTS

1 teaspoon chili powder (plus more for garnish)

3 lbs. parsnips, peeled and chopped

2 tablespoons olive oil

3 cups whole milk

2 bay leaves

Pinch of salt

1 stick butter

1 teaspoon pepper

¼ cup pistachios, shelled and crushed

Roasted Parsnip Puree with Chili-Dusted Pistachios

SERVINGS: 5 TO 7 • ACTIVE TIME: 30 MINUTES • TOTAL TIME: 2 HOURS

Roasting parsnips brings out the vegetable's natural sweetness and accents the slight heat of the chili powder for an irresistible side dish.

1 Preheat oven to 425°F.

2 Toss the pistachios and chili powder together and put aside.

3 Toss the peeled parsnips in olive oil and place on a baking sheet. Roast for 35 minutes or until golden brown and slightly caramelized.

4 Place a large saucepan over medium-high heat. Add the roasted parsnips, milk, and bay leaves.

5 Bring the mixture to a boil, then reduce heat to low and simmer for 20 minutes until the parsnips are very tender.

6 Strain the mixture through a mesh strainer, reserving the milk. Discard the bay leaves.

7 Place the parsnips in a blender with the salt and a tablespoon of the milk.

8 Blend well, adding additional milk as necessary. Add 1 tablespoon of butter at a time until you reach the desired consistency.

9 To serve, place in bowls and top with the chili powder and pistachios.

1 Preheat oven to 425°F.

2 In a frying pan over medium heat, cook the bacon until browned.

3 Using a slotted spoon, remove the bacon, set aside, and reserve the grease.

4 Place the squash on a baking sheet, drizzle with olive oil, and bake for 15 minutes.

5 Remove the pan from the oven and add the corn, garlic, peppers, onion, and thyme.

6 Pour the bacon grease over the vegetables and cook for 25 to 35 minutes, or until caramelized and softened.

7 Place the succotash in a serving bowl and season to taste.

INGREDIENTS

½ lb. bacon, diced

3 cups butternut squash, diced

3 tablespoons olive oil

4 cups corn

4 garlic cloves, minced

2 red peppers, diced

1 medium onion, diced

2 teaspoons fresh thyme

Salt and pepper, to taste

Roasted Cauliflower with Pineapple-Chili Sauce and Pine Nuts

SERVINGS: 4 TO 6 • ACTIVE TIME: 15 MINUTES • TOTAL TIME: 1 HOUR

The sweet, nutty, and spicy side dish is certain to become one of your favorite turkey pairings.

INGREDIENTS

2 cayenne chilies, stems removed

2 new mexico chilies, stems removed

1 cup pineapple, diced

2 garlic cloves, minced

3 tablespoons rice wine vinegar

¼ cup sugar

½ cup pineapple juice

Pinch of salt, plus more to taste

2 heads of cauliflower

2 tablespoons olive oil

3 tablespoons butter

½ cup pine nuts

1 Preheat the oven to 425°F.

2 In a blender, puree the chilies, pineapple, garlic, vinegar, sugar, and pineapple juice.

3 Strain the mixture through a fine sieve and discard the solids. Season with salt.

4 Cut the cauliflower into bite-sized florets. Toss the cauliflower in a bowl with the oil and pinch of salt.

5 Place in the oven and roast until golden and dark brown, about 25 to 35 minutes.

6 Toss the cauliflower in a bowl with the butter. Add the sauce and top with pine nuts.

Roasted Root Vegetables

SERVINGS: 4 TO 6 • **ACTIVE TIME: 20 MINUTES** • **TOTAL TIME: 60 MINUTES**

This recipe is a great way to cook a variety of root vegetables at once. The rosemary helps bring out the natural sweetness of the vegetables as they cook.

INGREDIENTS

2 small parsnips, trimmed and scrubbed clean

1 turnip, trimmed and scrubbed clean

4 small beets, trimmed and scrubbed clean

4 medium carrots, trimmed and scrubbed clean

½ onion, cut into slices

1 small bulb fennel, trimmed and cut into slivers

¼ cup olive oil

Salt and pepper, to taste

2 teaspoons dried rosemary, crumbled

1 Preheat the oven to 400°F.

2 Cut the cleaned vegetables into strips.

3 In a large bowl, combine the vegetables and olive oil. Toss to coat and season with salt and pepper.

4 Put the vegetables in a cast-iron skillet or baking dish and sprinkle with rosemary.

5 Put in the oven and bake for about 40 minutes, turning the vegetables over after the first 20 minutes. Serve warm.

NOTE: For a unique flavor, add basil, thyme, marjoram, tarragon, and lavender to embrace all the tastes of the garden.

Ratatouille

This twist on a French classic uses eggplant instead of zucchini for a more robust flavor.

1 Heat half the olive oil in a cast-iron skillet over medium-high heat. Add the garlic and eggplant and cook, stirring, until pieces are coated with oil and softened, about 2 minutes.

2 Reduce the heat to medium and add the peppers and remaining oil, while stirring. Cover the skillet and let cook for 15 minutes, stirring every so often. If the mix seems too dry, add a little more olive oil.

3 Once the eggplant and peppers are tender, add the tomatoes and stir to combine. Remove the lid and cook, stirring occasionally, until the eggplant and peppers are soft and the tomatoes are wilted. Remove the skillet from the heat, season with salt and pepper, and let sit for at least 1 hour. Reheat and serve.

INGREDIENTS

⅓ cup olive oil

6 garlic cloves, minced

1 medium eggplant, cut into bite-sized cubes

2 bell peppers, seeded and diced

4 tomatoes, seeded and chopped

Salt and pepper, to taste

NOTE: To substitute zucchini for the eggplant, use 1 small zucchini cut into half-moons. Add the zucchini with the peppers.

Grilled Yellow Squash and Zucchini

SERVINGS: 8 TO 10 • ACTIVE TIME: 15 MINUTES • TOTAL TIME: 35 MINUTES

This recipe is a great way to use up the bounty of squash and zucchini that comes every summer.

INGREDIENTS

2 medium yellow squash, cut into rounds

4 medium zucchini, cut into rounds

¼ cup olive oil

Sea salt and black pepper, to taste

1 Preheat your gas or charcoal grill to medium-high heat.

2 Place the vegetables, olive oil, salt, and pepper in a bowl, toss to coat, and set aside.

3 Once the grill reaches 400°F to 500°F, place the vegetables on the grill. Cook until tender, about 10 to 15 minutes, flipping once halfway through.

4 Remove from grill and serve.

Roasted Cauliflower

Roasting cauliflower accentuates its somewhat sweet, nutty flavor. Season it with warm, earthy spices like cumin and turmeric, and you have a delicious alternative to a starchy side.

1 Preheat the oven to 425°F.

2 In a bowl, combine the oil, salt, pepper, and spices and whisk thoroughly.

3 Cut the cauliflower into bite-sized pieces. Place in a cast-iron skillet and brush with the oil mixture.

4 Put the skillet in the oven and roast for about 20 minutes, turning the pieces over after 10 minutes.

5 Serve with a side of crème fraîche or sour cream, if desired.

INGREDIENTS

1½ tablespoons olive oil

1 teaspoon salt

Freshly ground pepper

½ teaspoon ground cumin

½ teaspoon ground coriander

½ teaspoon turmeric

¼ teaspoon cayenne pepper

1 medium head of cauliflower, stem and green leaves removed

Crème fraîche or sour cream, to serve

Glazed Carrots

SERVINGS: 4 • ACTIVE TIME: 20 MINUTES • TOTAL TIME: 40 MINUTES

This glaze helps highlight the natural sweetness of the carrots.

INGREDIENTS

1½ lbs. carrots

¾ cup water

4 tablespoons butter

2 tablespoons sugar

Salt, to taste

Parsley, chopped, for garnish

1 Peel and trim the carrots.

2 Put the carrots in a cast-iron skillet with the water, butter, and sugar. Bring to a boil over medium-high heat.

3 Once boiling, reduce the heat to low and simmer for another 10 minutes, stirring occasionally.

4 When carrots are tender, sprinkle with salt, garnish with the parsley, and serve.

Marvelous Mushrooms

Sautéing mushrooms in a cast-iron skillet with lots of butter yields a rich, earthy stew that complements a well-prepared turkey.

1 Heat a cast-iron skillet over medium-high heat and add the butter. Once melted, add the mushrooms. Cook, while stirring, until the mushrooms begin to soften, about 5 minutes. Reduce the heat to low and let the mushrooms simmer, stirring occasionally until they cook down, about 15 to 20 minutes.

2 Add the vermouth and stir. Season with salt and pepper. Simmer until the mushrooms begin to fall apart. Serve hot.

INGREDIENTS

6 tablespoons butter, cut into pieces

1 lb. mushrooms, cut into slices

1 teaspoon vermouth

Salt and pepper, to taste

NOTE: There are many kinds of mushrooms available, so mix and match them as you desire.

Spinach and Shallots

SERVINGS: 6 TO 8 • ACTIVE TIME: 25 MINUTES • TOTAL TIME: 40 MINUTES

Using shallots instead of the usual garlic and onions keeps the spinach flavor bright in this quick-cooking dish.

INGREDIENTS

3 tablespoons olive oil

4 large shallots, sliced thin

2 lbs. fresh spinach, tough stems removed, leaves rinsed and thoroughly dried

1 tablespoon balsamic vinegar

Salt and pepper, to taste

1 Heat a cast-iron skillet over medium-high heat. Add olive oil and shallots and cook while stirring until shallots are translucent, about 2 minutes.

2 Add the spinach and cook, stirring until all the leaves are coated, about 2 or 3 minutes. The spinach will start to wilt quickly. Turn the heat to low and cover the skillet to steam-cook the leaves.

3 When the spinach is wilted and still bright green, splash with the balsamic vinegar and shake to evenly coat. Season with salt and pepper and serve.

Stuffed Portobello Caps

SERVINGS: 4 • **ACTIVE TIME: 25 MINUTES** • **TOTAL TIME: 25 MINUTES**

The mushroom and tomato combo is so good, you'll be tempted to make this the main course.

1 Preheat your gas or charcoal grill to medium heat. Remove stems and gills from mushrooms.

2 Once the grill reaches 400°F, brush the mushrooms with the oil and grill for 2 minutes on each side, or until softened. Remove from heat and use paper towels to remove excess moisture from the insides of the caps.

3 Fill the caps with the tomatoes, garlic, mozzarella, and onions. Grill stuffing-side up for another 6 to 8 minutes.

4 Remove from heat and top with bread crumbs. Serve immediately.

INGREDIENTS

4 large portobello mushrooms

3 teaspoons olive oil

½ cup grape tomatoes, diced

1 garlic clove, minced

2 tablespoons fresh mozzarella

1 green onion, thinly sliced

1 small white onion, diced

1 red bell pepper, diced

1 loaf of sourdough bread, toasted and chopped into fine crumbs

Crazy Good Cabbage

SERVINGS: 4 TO 6 • ACTIVE TIME: 30 MINUTES • TOTAL TIME: 1 HOUR

This recipe is a great way to spice up cabbage, as the onions and cayenne add a whole new dimension.

INGREDIENTS

2 tablespoons olive oil

1 medium head of cabbage, cored and shredded

1 green bell pepper, seeds and ribs removed, diced

1 medium onion, diced

3 cups fresh tomatoes, seeds removed, chopped

1 ear of corn, kernels removed

8 oz. of canned corn, drained

1 teaspoon cayenne pepper

Salt and pepper, to taste

1 Heat a cast-iron skillet over medium-high heat and add the oil. Add cabbage, peppers, and onion and cook, while stirring , for about 3 minutes, or until the onion is translucent. Add the tomatoes, corn, and cayenne and stir. Season with salt and pepper.

2 Cover, reduce the heat to low, and simmer until the cabbage is cooked through, stirring occassionally, about 30 minutes. Serve hot.

Green Beans Almondine

SERVINGS: 6 TO 8 • ACTIVE TIME: 10 MINUTES • TOTAL TIME: 20 MINUTES

This French take on classic cooked green beans adds a hint of sweetness to your dinner that is balanced by a dash of lemon juice.

1 Place the green beans in a large pot of boiling salted water. Cook until al dente, about 5 minutes. Immediately place the green beans into an ice water bath. Remove and set aside.

2 Next, heat a large cast-iron skillet over medium heat and add the almonds. Stir for about 30 seconds until lightly toasted. Mix in the butter and lemon juice. When the butter is melted, add all of the beans and sauté for about 2 minutes, stirring to coat the beans.

3 Season to taste with salt and pepper and serve.

INGREDIENTS

1 lb. fresh green beans, trimmed

⅓ cup slivered almonds

3 tablespoons butter

1 teaspoon lemon juice

Salt and pepper, to taste

Sautéed Cherry Tomatoes

SERVINGS: 4 • ACTIVE TIME: 25 MINUTES • TOTAL TIME: 25 MINUTES

Fresh rosemary adds lovely fragrance to this simple dish.

INGREDIENTS

1 pint cherry tomatoes

1 tablespoon olive oil

1 garlic clove, minced

½ teaspoon salt

Black pepper, to taste

2 teaspoons fresh rosemary

1 Preheat the oven to 450°F.

2 In a bowl, toss the cherry tomatoes with the oil, garlic, salt, and pepper. Place in a baking dish or cast-iron skillet.

3 Roast in the oven for 10 minutes. Then, remove from the oven, and move the tomatoes around to ensure even roasting. Return to the oven and roast for another 5 minutes. Remove, stir, and sprinkle with the rosemary. Then return to the oven for another 5 minutes until the tomatoes are charred.

4 Season with additional salt and pepper if desired, and serve.

Fried Okra

Breaded in cornmeal and fried in a cast-iron skillet, these okra are better than french fries and much healthier.

1 Preheat the oven to 225°F. In a large bowl, whisk together the egg and milk until thoroughly combined. In another bowl, whisk together the cornmeal, flour, salt, and pepper.

2 Add the okra to the egg mixture and toss until coated. Add half of the dry mixture and toss to coat. Then add the remaining cornmeal-and-flour mixture and toss again to coat evenly.

3 Heat the oil in a cast-iron skillet over medium-high heat.

4 Place the breaded okra into the hot oil and fry them, turning gently with a slotted spoon. Cook until golden, about 3 minutes. Transfer the fried pieces to a platter covered with paper towels and place in the oven to keep warm. Continue frying in batches until all are cooked.

5 Season with salt and red pepper flakes, if desired, and serve.

INGREDIENTS

1 egg, beaten

½ cup milk

1 cup cornmeal

1 tablespoon flour

¾ teaspoon salt

½ teaspoon freshly ground black pepper

1 lb. fresh okra, sliced into ½-inch-thick rounds

2 cups canola oil

Sea salt, to taste (optional)

Red pepper flakes, to taste (optional)

Sautéed Greens

SERVINGS: 4 TO 6 • ACTIVE TIME: 20 MINUTES • TOTAL TIME: 30 MINUTES

The red pepper flakes and Swiss chard combine beautifully with the kale in this dish.

INGREDIENTS

2 tablespoons olive oil

2 garlic cloves, sliced thin

½ teaspoon red pepper flakes

1 bunch of Swiss chard, tough ends removed, leaves chopped

1 bunch of kale, tough stems removed, leaves chopped

Salt and pepper, to taste

1 Heat the oil in a cast-iron skillet over medium-high heat. Add the garlic. Cook until garlic begins to bounce, about 1 to 2 minutes. Add the red pepper flakes.

2 Add the greens, stirring gently to expose them to the hot oil. Reduce the heat to medium and continue to stir as the greens cook down.

3 Once cooked down, allow the greens to cook over medium heat, stirring occasionally, until wilted and soft, about 5 to 10 minutes. If necessary, add more oil to the pan while cooking.

4 When the greens are soft and cooked down, transfer to a bowl, season with salt and pepper, and serve.

Casseroles, Spuds, and Breads

Green Bean and Mushroom Soup Casserole

SERVINGS: 6 TO 8 • ACTIVE TIME: 30 MINUTES
TOTAL TIME: 1 HOUR AND 20 MINUTES

MUSHROOM SOUP INGREDIENTS

½ lb. bacon, diced

1 lb. mushrooms, cleaned and sliced

3 garlic cloves, minced

3 sprigs thyme

Pinch of salt

1 teaspoon black pepper

2 tablespoons butter

¼ cup all-purpose flour

1 cup turkey stock (see page 86)

1 cup water

1½ cups whole milk

1 teaspoon soy sauce

1 cup heavy cream

MUSHROOM SOUP DIRECTIONS

1 Cook the bacon in a pan over medium heat until brown.

2 With a slotted spoon, remove the bacon and set on paper towels to drain. Add mushrooms, garlic, thyme, salt, and pepper to the pan.

3 Sauté for about 5 minutes or until the mushroom mixture starts to break down and brown.

4 Add butter and flour to the pan, stir, and cook for about 2 minutes, being sure not to burn the flour mixture.

5 Add the turkey stock and water, stir, and let simmer for 2 to 5 minutes.

6 Add the milk, soy sauce, and cream and stir. If the mixture is too thick, add a small amount of water until soup is a creamy consistency that coats the back of a spoon. Set soup aside to cool.

This Thanksgiving classic takes on a savory flavor thanks to the addition of mushrooms.

GREEN BEAN CASSEROLE DIRECTIONS

1 In a pot, bring the oil to 375°F.

2 Preheat oven to 350°F.

3 Combine the cornstarch and flour in a bowl and set aside.

4 Coat the shallots in the flour-and-cornstarch mixture.

5 Place the shallots in the oil and cook until golden brown. Remove, set on paper towels to drain, and sprinkle with the salt.

6 Grease a 9 x 13–inch baking dish. Put the green beans in the baking dish and pour the mushroom soup over the top. Add the bacon reserved from the mushroom soup, place in the oven, and bake for 15 minutes.

7 Remove the dish, place the fried shallots on top of the casserole evenly, and put the casserole back in the oven for an additional 10 to 15 minutes, checking regularly to prevent the shallots from burning.

GREEN BEAN CASSEROLE INGREDIENTS

2 cups canola oil for frying

½ cup cornstarch

½ cup all-purpose flour

4 shallots, sliced

Pinch of salt

5 cups of green beans (fresh preferred)

2½ cups of mushroom soup

1 teaspoon black pepper

Loaded Potato Casserole

SERVINGS: 5 TO 7 • **ACTIVE TIME: 20 MINUTES** • **TOTAL TIME: 55 MINUTES**

Roasting the potatoes gives this dish a smoky flavor that goes well with the sour cream and cheese.

1. Preheat oven to 400°F.

2. Fry the bacon in a pan over medium heat until brown.

3. Using a slotted spoon, remove the bacon, and drain on paper towels. Reserve the grease.

4. On a baking sheet, place the potatoes, sprinkle with salt to taste, and cover with bacon grease. Bake for 35 minutes, or until tender and brown.

5. When the potatoes are done allow them to cool for 10 minutes.

6. Put potatoes in a large bowl with cheese, chives, garlic powder, mayonnaise, sour cream, salt, pepper, and diced bacon. Mix well and serve.

INGREDIENTS

½ lb. bacon, diced

5 cups potatoes, peeled and sliced thin

3 teaspoons salt, plus more to taste

½ cup cheddar cheese, shredded

¼ cup chives

2 teaspoons garlic powder

½ cup mayonnaise

½ cup sour cream

1 teaspoon black pepper

Home-Style Baked Beans

SERVINGS: 6 TO 8 • ACTIVE TIME: 30 MINUTES • TOTAL TIME: 1½ TO 2 HOURS

The Dijon really makes this dish, as it adds just the right amount of kick.

INGREDIENTS

6 strips thick-cut bacon

½ onion, diced

½ cup bell pepper, ribs and seeds removed, diced

1 teaspoon salt, plus more to taste

2 (15.5 oz.) cans of pinto beans, rinsed and drained

1 cup barbecue sauce

1 teaspoon Dijon mustard

2 tablespoons dark brown sugar

Fresh black pepper, to taste

1 Preheat the oven to 325°F.

2 Warm a cast-iron skillet over medium heat and cook half the bacon pieces until they are just starting to brown, about 8 minutes. Transfer to a plate lined with paper towels to drain.

3 Add the remaining pieces of bacon to the pan, turn up the heat, and cook until pieces are browned. Reduce the heat to medium. Add the onion and pepper and cook, stirring occasionally, until the vegetables soften, about 8 minutes.

4 Add the salt, beans, barbecue sauce, mustard, and brown sugar. Stir, season with additional salt and pepper, and cook until the liquid just starts to simmer.

5 Lay the partially cooked pieces of bacon on top and transfer the skillet to the oven.

6 Bake for 1 hour. The bacon should be crisp and browned, and the sauce should be thick. Be careful not to overcook the beans, as they will start to dry out.

7 Remove from the oven and allow to cool slightly before serving.

Bacon Macaroni and Cheese

SERVINGS: 6 • ACTIVE TIME: 40 MINUTES
TOTAL TIME: 1 HOUR AND 30 MINUTES

Be sure to undercook the pasta when preparing this; otherwise, it will become a mess once baked.

1 Preheat the oven to 375°F. Butter a 3-quart casserole dish and set aside.

2 Heat the largest skillet you have over medium heat for 2 to 3 minutes. Add 2 tablespoons of the butter and heat on medium-high. Once melted, add the bread crumbs and salt and pepper. Cook, stirring frequently, until the crumbs are a deep golden color, about 6 minutes. Transfer them to a bowl. Once the bread crumbs have cooled, toss with the parsley.

3 Return the skillet to the stove and turn the heat to medium. Add the bacon and cook until the fat renders and it turns crispy, about 8 minutes. Using a slotted spoon, transfer the bacon bits to a small bowl. Drain the fat from the skillet into a measuring cup. Then, return just enough fat to it to cover the bottom of the skillet in a thin film. Add the jalapeños, cooking until they soften, about 5 minutes. Remove from the heat.

4 Melt the remaining 4 tablespoons butter in a medium saucepan over medium heat. Once it has melted, add the flour and whisk into a paste. Cook, stirring continuously, until the mixture turns a slightly golden color, about 2 to 3 minutes. Slowly pour the milk into the pan, whisking continuously to create a roux. Once added, cook the mixture, whisking constantly, until thickened, about 5 minutes. Add salt, black pepper, the nutmeg, cayenne pepper, 1 cup of the pepper jack, and ¾ cup each of the Gruyère and Parmigiano and stir until the cheeses are melted. Remove from the heat and set aside.

5 Bring a large pot of water to a boil. Once boiling, add 1 tablespoon of salt for every 4 cups of water, and stir. Add the pasta, stirring for the first minute to prevent any sticking. Cook the pasta 4 fewer minutes than directed on the package, so that the pasta will still be too firm to eat. Drain the pasta, rinse under cold water, and let drain. Return the pasta to its pot, add the cheese sauce, bacon bits, jalapeños, and any remaining oil in the skillet, and toss well.

6 Pour the mixture into the prepared baking dish. Sprinkle the remaining pepper jack, Gruyère, and Parmigiano over the top. Bake until bubbling and slightly browned on top, about 30 minutes. Remove the dish from the oven and turn on the broiler. Sprinkle the bread crumbs evenly over the top and return to the oven for 1 to 2 minutes. Remove from the oven and let cool for 10 minutes before serving.

INGREDIENTS

6 tablespoons unsalted butter, plus more for the baking dish

1 cup panko bread crumbs

Salt and freshly ground black pepper, to taste

¼ cup fresh parsley leaves, minced

5 to 6 oz. bacon, diced

2 jalapeño peppers, seeded and minced

¼ cup all-purpose flour

2¾ cups whole milk

¼ teaspoon freshly grated nutmeg

¼ teaspoon cayenne pepper

2 cups (about 8 oz.) pepper jack cheese, grated

1 cup (about 6 oz.) Gruyère cheese, grated

1¼ cups Parmigiano-Reggiano cheese, grated

1 lb. elbow macaroni

Sweet Potato Casserole

Sweet, syrupy, and crunchy, you'll hear the couch calling after you enjoy this rich, delicious casserole.

Place the sweet potatoes in a large pot and fill with water until just covered. Bring the pot to a boil, reduce the heat, and allow the potatoes to simmer for about 15 minutes or until tender. Drain and allow to cool.

Preheat the oven to 375°F and prepare a large casserole dish with cooking spray.

Return the potatoes to the large pot and add the sugar, butter, salt, and vanilla extract. Mash the sweet potatoes with a potato masher, then stir in ¼ of cup pecans.

Add the potato mixture to the casserole dish and spread out evenly. Sprinkle the remaining pecans and the marshmallows evenly on the top, then bake for 25 minutes until golden and melted.

INGREDIENTS

2½ lbs. sweet potatoes, peeled and cut into 1-inch cubes

¾ cup brown sugar, packed

⅓ cup butter, softened

1½ teaspoons salt

½ teaspoon vanilla extract

½ cup pecans, chopped

Cooking spray

2 cups miniature marshmallows

Casseroles, Spuds, and Breads

Pancetta and Potatoes Au Gratin

SERVINGS 6 TO 8 • ACTIVE TIME: 10 MINUTES
TOTAL TIME: 1 HOUR AND 40 MINUTES

When you take something as delicious as pancetta and add it to the classic cheesy potato gratin, you end up with a dish that always disappears too fast.

1 Preheat the oven to 350°F.

2 Place the potatoes, milk, cream, garlic powder, salt, and pepper in a bowl.

3 Grease a 3-quart baking pan and put a layer of the potato mixture on the bottom. Place half of the pancetta, butter, and cheddar on top of the layer of potatoes and spread to cover. Repeat this process until the potatoes are gone.

4 Top with additional cheddar cheese and cover the dish with foil.

5 Bake for 1 hour. Remove the cover and bake for an additional 30 minutes.

INGREDIENTS

5 cups potatoes, peeled and sliced thin

¼ cup milk

¼ cup cream

2 teaspoons garlic powder

3 teaspoons salt

1 teaspoon black pepper

4 oz. pancetta, diced

3 tablespoons unsalted butter, cut into cubes

1½ cups cheddar cheese, shredded, plus more for topping

Roasted Fingerling Potatoes with Thyme Butter

SERVINGS: 4 • ACTIVE TIME: 5 MINUTES • TOTAL TIME: 1 HOUR

This dish sounds simple, but its flavor is second to none. Don't be stingy with the salt, as it will really amplify all the ingredients.

INGREDIENTS

½ stick unsalted butter at room temperature

3 teaspoons salt, plus more to taste

1 tablespoon fresh thyme leaves

1½ lbs. fingerling potatoes, rinsed

2 tablespoons olive oil at room temperature

1 Preheat oven to 400°F.

2 Meanwhile, place the butter, salt to taste, and thyme in a bowl and beat until well combined, about 1 minutes.

3 Place the thyme butter in a container and refrigerate for 1 hour.

4 In a large bowl, toss the potatoes, salt, and olive oil together and mix well.

5 Place potatoes in a baking dish and bake until golden brown, about 40 minutes.

6 When the potatoes are ready, transfer them to a bowl, toss in thyme butter, and serve.

Blue Cheese Mashed Potatoes

SERVINGS: 4 TO 6 • ACTIVE TIME: 5 MINUTES • TOTAL TIME: 40 MINUTES

Using a high-quality blue cheese like Roquefort or Stilton will make this simple recipe one to remember.

Peel and dice the potatoes.

Place potatoes in a pot of cold, salted water and bring to boil over medium-high heat. Once boiling, reduce heat to medium-low and cook until fork tender.

Once tender, drain the potatoes and place in a large bowl. Add butter, salt, pepper, blue cheese, milk, and cream to the bowl, mash to the desired consistency, and serve.

INGREDIENTS

3 lbs. russet potatoes

½ stick unsalted butter

3 teaspoons salt

1 teaspoon pepper

1 lb. blue cheese

⅓ cup milk

¼ cup cream

Chipotle and Maple Mashed Sweet Potatoes

SERVINGS: 5 TO 7 • ACTIVE TIME: 10 MINUTES • TOTAL TIME: 50 MINUTES

The sweetness in this dish balances out the smokiness of the chipotle peppers.

INGREDIENTS

5 cups of sweet potatoes, peeled and diced

3 teaspoons salt

3 tablespoons unsalted butter, cut into cubes

¼ cup cream

¼ cup milk

1 teaspoon black pepper

2 teaspoons garlic powder

½ cup of pure maple syrup

1 (4 oz.) can of chipotle peppers in adobo (add more or less to taste)

1 Place the sweet potatoes in a pot of cold, salted water. Place on medium-high heat and bring to a boil. Cook until fork tender.

2 Drain the potatoes. Add butter, cream, milk, pepper, garlic powder, maple syrup, and chipotle peppers.

3 With an immersion blender or potato masher, mix until light and creamy. Season to taste and serve.

Bone Marrow Mashed Potatoes

SERVINGS: 6 TO 8 • ACTIVE TIME: 25 MINUTES • TOTAL TIME: 1 HOUR

Sneak some bone marrow into this side dish for a unique new taste.

1 Preheat the oven to 375°F. Place one of the racks in the center of the oven.

2 Place the marrow bones on a baking sheet. Transfer to the oven, and then cook for about 15 minutes, until the marrow is nicely browned. Remove from the oven and let stand.

3 While the marrow bones are roasting, place the potatoes in a large stockpot and fill with water until the potatoes are submerged by 1 inch.

4 Place the stockpot on the stove. Boil for about 20 minutes, until you can pierce the potatoes with a fork. Remove from heat and drain the water, leaving the potatoes in the pot.

5 Using a potato masher or fork, mash the potatoes slowly. Gradually add the half-and-half and butter as you mash, tasting until arrive at the perfect blend of creamy, buttery, mashed potatoes.

6 Scoop the marrow from the bones and add to the potatoes. Mix in the rosemary. Season with salt and pepper and serve warm.

INGREDIENTS

8 Yukon Gold
potatoes, peeled
and cut into quarters

4 to 6 large
beef marrow bones,
halved lengthwise

½ cup half-and-half

½ cup (1 stick)
unsalted butter,
softened

1 teaspoon
fresh rosemary,
minced

Sea salt and coarsely
ground black pepper,
to taste

INGREDIENTS

2 premade piecrusts

2 lbs. Yukon Gold
potatoes, peeled

1¼ cups crème fraîche

1 tablespoon kosher salt

½ teaspoon
black pepper

Pinch of grated nutmeg

2 garlic cloves, crushed

2 teaspoons fresh
thyme, chopped

1 egg yolk

1 tablespoon
half-and-half

French Potato Tart

SERVINGS: 4 TO 6 • ACTIVE TIME: 45 MINUTES • TOTAL TIME: 2 HOURS

The crème fraîche blankets very thin potato slices much like a traditional au gratin.

Preheat the oven to 400°F.

Using a very sharp knife, a mandoline, or a spiralizer, slice the potatoes as thin as possible.

In a bowl, combine the crème fraîche, salt, pepper, nutmeg, garlic, and thyme. Stir to combine.

Add the potato slices and fold gently to cover with the crème.

On a lightly floured surface, roll out the bottom crust so that it is just larger than the bottom of the pan and lay it in a cast-iron skillet.

Layer the potato slices in the crust, creating even, tight layers. Once all the potatoes are used up, use a rubber spatula to scrape the cream mixture into the pie. Tap the edges of the skillet to distribute the mixture evenly.

On a lightly floured surface, roll out the top crust and crimp the edges with the bottom crust to seal. Blend the egg yolk with the half-and-half and brush the mixture over the top crust. Cut 4 to 5 slits in the middle.

Put the skillet in the oven and bake for 15 minutes. Reduce temperature to 350°F and continue to bake for 1 hour, or until potatoes are tender.

Serve hot or at room temperature.

Roasted Red Potatoes

As easy as they are delicious, these potatoes are here to lighten your load in the kitchen.

INGREDIENTS

12 to 14 small red potatoes, scrubbed clean

2 to 3 tablespoons olive oil

Freshly ground pepper and coarse sea salt, to taste

Fresh parsley, chopped, for garnish (optional)

Rosemary, for garnish (optional)

1 Preheat the oven to 375°F.

2 In a bowl, drizzle oil over the potatoes. Grind some fresh pepper on the potatoes. Put them in a baking dish or cast-iron skillet to form a single layer. Sprinkle with sea salt.

3 Bake in the oven for 25 to 40 minutes or until the potatoes are cooked through, turning halfway through to ensure even cooking. Serve hot with rosemary or parsley as garnish.

Classic Potato Salad

This barbecue classic goes great with a smoked or grilled turkey.

1 Place the potatoes in a large saucepan and cover with water. Bring to a boil and cook for 20 minutes, or until tender. Drain and let cool. Then, dice the potatoes. Set aside.

2 Combine the mayonnaise, apple cider vinegar, sugar, mustard, salt, and spices in a large bowl. Then add the potatoes, celery, and onion.

3 Stir in the eggs and dust with paprika on top.

INGREDIENTS

8 medium potatoes, peeled

1½ cups mayonnaise

2 tablespoons sugar

1 tablespoon mustard

1 teaspoon salt

2 tablespoons apple cider vinegar

1 teaspoon garlic powder

½ teaspoon black pepper

2 celery stalks, chopped

1 cup onion, minced

5 hard-boiled eggs, chopped

Paprika, to taste

Potato Pancakes

SERVINGS: 6 • ACTIVE TIME: 1½ HOURS • TOTAL TIME: 2 HOURS

The key to great potato pancakes is getting as much liquid out of the grated potatoes and onions as possible.

INGREDIENTS

6 large russet potatoes, washed and peeled

1 large onion

3 eggs, beaten

¼ to ½ cup bread crumbs

Salt and pepper, to taste

1 cup canola or vegetable oil

1 Using a hand grater or a food processor with a shredding attachment, grate the potatoes onto a large baking dish. Then transfer to a colander in the sink.

2 Grate the onion or use a knife to mince very finely. Put the onion into a bowl.

3 Squeeze as much liquid out of the potatoes as possible. Take half of the grated potatoes, mix them with the onions, and process the mixture in a food processor or blender to create a rough puree. Don't overblend or chop, as the mix will get too starchy.

4 Put the puree in a separate colander to drain. Let both colanders drain for another 20 to 30 minutes. Push down on both to release more liquid and squeeze them again before continuing with the recipe.

5 Combine the contents of the colanders a large bowl. Add the eggs and bread crumbs. Stir to thoroughly combine. Season with salt and pepper.

Heat a cast-iron skillet over medium-high heat and add the oil. Take rounded spoonfuls of the potato mix and place them in the oil. Cook for about 3 minutes a side. The pancakes should be golden brown on the outside, and cooked through on the inside. You may need to adjust the temperature of the oil to get the right cooking temperature, if you have more than three in the skillet at once.

Transfer with a slotted spoon to a plate lined with paper towels. Keep warm until ready to eat. Season with additional salt and pepper.

Sweet Potato Pancakes

SERVINGS: 6 • ACTIVE TIME: 1 HOUR • TOTAL TIME: 1 HOUR AND 30 MINUTES

Sweet potatoes aren't as moist as russet potatoes, so they don't require as much draining time, but they need to be chopped finer for the batter. Experiment until you get the right consistency.

INGREDIENTS

6 large sweet potatoes, washed and peeled

1 large onion

3 eggs, beaten

½ cup matzoh meal

½ teaspoon sugar

Salt and freshly ground pepper, to taste

1 cup canola or vegetable oil

1 Using a hand grater or a food processor with a shredding attachment, grate the potatoes onto a large baking dish. Then transfer to a colander in the sink.

2 Grate the onion or use a knife to mince very finely. Put the grated onion into a bowl.

3 Squeeze as much liquid out of the potatoes as possible.

4 Combine the potatoes and onion and begin processing in a food processor or blender to turn the vegetables into a rough puree. Don't overblend or chop, as the mix will get too starchy.

5 Squeeze the puree through a fine sieve to get out excess liquid, then let the mix sit and drain on its own for about 20 to 30 minutes.

6 Put the puree into a large bowl. Add the eggs, matzoh meal, and sugar. Stir to thoroughly combine. Season with salt and pepper.

7 Heat a cast-iron skillet over medium-high heat and add the oil. Take rounded spoonfuls of the potato mix and place them in the oil. Cook for about 3 minutes a side. The pancakes should be golden brown on the outside and cooked through. You may need to adjust the oil to get the right cooking temperature if you have more than three in the skillet at once.

8 Once cooked, transfer with a slotted spoon to a plate lined with paper towels. Keep warm until ready to eat. Season with additional salt and pepper.

NOTE: Serve with pesto or refried beans, or put some on a baking sheet, top with grated mozzarella, and broil for a couple of minutes to melt the cheese.

Dinner Rolls

These are so easy and tasty that you'll never settle for store-bought rolls again.

1 In a small bowl, combine ½ cup of the warm milk and the sugar. Sprinkle the yeast, stir, and set aside so the yeast can proof, about 10 minutes.

2 While the yeast is proofing, melt the butter in a cast-iron skillet over low to medium heat. Remove from heat when melted.

3 Once the yeast mixture is frothy, stir in 3 tablespoons of the melted butter, the remaining milk, the salt, and the eggs. Then, stir in the flour, until all ingredients are incorporated. Transfer to a lightly floured surface and knead the dough for 5 to 10 minutes until it is soft, springy, and elastic.

4 Grease a large mixing bowl. Place the ball of dough in the bowl and cover loosely with plastic wrap. Place in a naturally warm, draft-free location, and let rise until doubled in size, about 45 minutes to 1 hour.

5 Prepare a lightly floured surface to work on. Punch down the dough in the bowl and transfer it to the floured surface. Warm the skillet with the butter until melted again, then remove from the heat.

6 Break off pieces of the dough, shaping them into balls with a 2-inch diameter. Roll the balls in the butter in the skillet.

7 Cover the skillet loosely with a clean dish towel, return to the warm, draft-free spot, and let the rolls rise until doubled in size, about 30 minutes. While they're rising, preheat the oven to 350°F.

8 Once the rolls have risen and the oven is ready, cover the skillet with aluminum foil and bake in the oven for 20 minutes. Remove the foil and finish cooking, about another 15 minutes or so, until the rolls are golden on top and are light and springy. Serve warm.

INGREDIENTS

1¼ cups whole milk, heated to 110°F

3 tablespoons sugar

1 tablespoon active dry yeast

1 stick of unsalted butter

¾ teaspoon salt

2 eggs at room temperature, lightly beaten

3½ cups cake or bread flour (not all-purpose flour)

Garlic and Rosemary Rolls

SERVINGS 6 TO 8 • **ACTIVE TIME: 1 HOUR AND 30 MINUTES**
TOTAL TIME: 3 HOURS

The rosemary in these rolls makes them nearly irresistible.

1 In a large bowl, mix the yeast, water, and sugar and let the yeast proof for about 10 minutes until foamy.

2 Add the melted butter, salt, garlic, and half the flour. Mix until a sticky dough forms. Continue to add flour, mixing to form a soft dough. Add the rosemary with the last addition of flour.

3 Coat the bottom and sides of a large mixing bowl (ceramic is best) with butter. Place the ball of dough in the bowl and cover loosely with plastic wrap. Place in a naturally warm, draft-free location, and let it rise until doubled in size, about 45 minutes to 1 hour.

4 Put a cast-iron skillet in the oven and preheat the oven to 400°F.

5 Transfer the dough to a lightly floured surface. Divide into 8 pieces and form into balls.

6 Remove the skillet from the oven and melt the butter in it. Place the rolls in the skillet, turning to cover them with butter. Wash the rolls with the beaten egg and season with sea salt.

7 Bake in the oven until golden and set, about 40 minutes.

INGREDIENTS

1 packet active dry yeast (2¼ teaspoons)

1 cup water (110°F to 115°F)

1 tablespoon sugar

1 tablespoon butter, melted

1 teaspoon sea salt, plus more to taste

2 garlic cloves, minced

4 cups flour

1 teaspoon fresh rosemary leaves, chopped

1 tablespoon butter

1 egg, lightly beaten

Biscuits

For fluffy buttermilk biscuits, you need to work with a very hot skillet. The golden brown crust on the bottom is as much of a delight as the airy, warm dough.

1 Preheat oven to 450° F.

2 In a large bowl, combine the flour, sugar, salt, and baking powder.

3 Using a fork or pastry knife, blend in 6 tablespoons of the butter to form a crumbly dough. Form a well in the middle and add ½ cup of the buttermilk. Stir to combine and form a stiff dough. If the mixture is too dry, add buttermilk 1 tablespoon at a time as necessary.

4 Put 2 tablespoons of butter in the skillet and put the skillet in the oven.

5 Put the dough on a lightly floured surface and press out to a thickness of about 1 inch. Cut out biscuits using an inverted water glass. Place the biscuits in the skillet and bake for about 10 minutes, until golden on the bottom.

INGREDIENTS

2 cups flour

1 teaspoon sugar

1 teaspoon salt

1 tablespoon baking powder

8 tablespoons butter, cut into pieces

½ cup buttermilk, plus 2 tablespoons

Desserts

Apple Crisp with Salted Oat Crumble

SERVINGS: 4 • ACTIVE TIME: 10 MINUTES • TOTAL TIME: 55 MINUTES

The sweetness of the apples with the crunchy texture of oats and the deep cinnamon flavor make this dessert irresistible. Don't be stingy with the salt; it brings out these flavors in a major way.

1 Preheat oven to 350°F.

2 In a medium bowl, mix together sugar, apples, and half of the cinnamon. Put the apple mixture into a greased 9 x 9–inch baking dish.

3 In a separate bowl, mix oats, flour, cinnamon, butter, and brown sugar.

4 Use a pastry cutter or your hands to break up the butter and mash the mixture together until it is combined and crumbly.

5 Spread the crumble mixture on top of the apple mixture. Season with the salt and bake uncovered for 40 to 45 minutes until brown. If desired, top with walnuts and serve with vanilla ice cream.

INGREDIENTS

3 tablespoons sugar

5 apples, peeled, cored and sliced

1 cup oats

¾ cup all-purpose flour

1 teaspoon cinnamon

½ cup cold butter

1 cup brown sugar

Salt, to taste

Walnuts, for topping (optional)

Vanilla ice cream (optional)

Pear and Cinnamon Bread Pudding with Salted Bourbon Caramel

SERVINGS: 4 • ACTIVE TIME: 20 MINUTES • TOTAL TIME: 55 MINUTES

Bread pudding alone is fantastic, but once you bring in the sweetness of pears and top it all with salted caramel sauce, you are in for a real treat.

1 Preheat oven to 350°F.

2 Place the sugar and water in a medium saucepan and cook over medium heat until the mixture becomes a dark amber color, about 10 to 15 minutes. Swirl the pan as it cooks but do not stir the mixture.

3 Remove from heat and whisk in cream, vanilla, salt, and bourbon. The mixture will produce a lot of steam, so be careful not to burn yourself. Set the salted caramel aside.

4 Tear bread into small pieces and place in a greased 9 x 9–inch baking dish.

5 In a mixing bowl, combine the butter, eggs, milk, sugar, cinnamon, and vanilla.

6 Pour the mixture over the bread and push the mixture down with a fork, making sure to soak all of the bread. Top with pear slices and bake for 40 to 45 minutes until the top is brown.

7 Once the bread pudding is done, top with salted caramel.

SALTED CARAMEL INGREDIENTS

1½ cups sugar

½ cup water

1 cup heavy cream

1 teaspoon
vanilla extract

3 teaspoons salt

2 tablespoons bourbon

BREAD PUDDING INGREDIENTS

6 cups stale bread

2 tablespoons unsalted
butter, melted

4 eggs, beaten

1¾ cup milk

¾ cup sugar

2 teaspoons cinnamon

1 teaspoon
vanilla extract

3 pears, peeled
and sliced

Blue Hubbard Squash Pie with Marshmallow Creme

SERVINGS: 8 • ACTIVE TIME: 20 MINUTES
TOTAL TIME: 3 HOURS AND 20 MINUTES

There are many other squashes than pumpkin that lend themselves to a fantastic pie, and the blue hubbard squash is the best of them all, despite its slightly odd appearance.

1 Preheat oven to 425°F.

2 In a small saucepan, bring the cream and marshmallow creme to a simmer while stirring. Remove from heat, place the mixture in a bowl, and refrigerate for 2 hours.

3 Slice the squash into quarters and place it on a baking sheet. Drizzle with oil and place in the oven for 40 to 45 minutes, or until the squash is very tender.

4 Let the squash cool for 15 minutes and scoop out the innards and seeds. Scoop the meat of the squash into a bowl and mash.

5 Measure out 2 cups of the mashed squash and save the rest for leftovers or a future preparation.

6 In a medium bowl, mix the sugar, milk, spices, butter, and eggs. Pour the mixture through a fine mesh strainer and place it in an unbaked piecrust.

7 Bake for 35 to 45 minutes until the mixture sets and a toothpick inserted into the center comes out clean.

8 Let the pie cool and then refrigerate for at least 4 hours. When you are ready to serve the pie, top it with the marshmallow creme.

INGREDIENTS

1 cup heavy cream

½ cup marshmallow creme, plus more for topping

1 blue hubbard squash (or squash of your choice)

1 tablespoon olive oil

1 cup white sugar

2 cups hot milk

½ teaspoon cinnamon

¼ teaspoon nutmeg

1 tablespoon unsalted butter

3 eggs

1 9-inch piecrust

PIE INGREDIENTS

1 (15 oz.) can pumpkin puree

1 (12 oz.) can evaporated milk

2 eggs, lightly beaten

¼ cup sugar

¼ cup 100% natural Grade B (dark) maple syrup

½ teaspoon salt

1 teaspoon cinnamon

¼ teaspoon ground ginger

¼ teaspoon ground nutmeg

1 tablespoon butter

1 tablespoon light brown sugar

1 12-inch piecrust

TOPPING INGREDIENTS

4 tablespoons butter, melted

¼ cup 100% natural Grade B (dark) maple syrup

Maple Pumpkin Pie

SERVINGS: 6 TO 8 • ACTIVE TIME: 30 MINUTES • TOTAL TIME: 2 HOURS

If you ever find yourself wishing pumpkin pie were sweeter, this is the dessert for you.

1 Preheat the oven to 400°F.

2 In a large bowl, combine the pumpkin puree, evaporated milk, eggs, sugar, maple syrup, salt, cinnamon, ginger, and nutmeg. Stir to combine thoroughly.

3 Put a cast-iron skillet over medium heat and melt the butter in it. Add the brown sugar and cook, stirring constantly, until sugar is dissolved, about 1 or 2 minutes. Carefully remove pan from heat.

4 Place the piecrust into the skillet over the sugar mixture. Fill the piecrust with the pumpkin mix.

5 Put the skillet in the oven and bake for 15 minutes, then reduce the heat to 325°F and bake an additional 30 to 45 minutes until the filling is firm and a toothpick inserted in the middle comes out clean. Don't overcook.

6 Make the maple topping by putting the butter and maple syrup in a bowl and stirring to thoroughly combine. Spoon the mixture and carefully spread over the top of the pie. Preheat the broiler to high. Place a rack on the top shelf of the oven. Broil the pie until the topping is just toasted, keeping an eye on it to be sure it doesn't burn, about 5 minutes. Cool slightly before serving.

Baked Apples

SERVINGS: 4 • ACTIVE TIME: 30 MINUTES • TOTAL TIME: 50 MINUTES

These are easy to make and are delicious served warm or at room temperature the next day. They're best with a side of vanilla ice cream or even maple Greek yogurt.

INGREDIENTS

4 firm apples

2 tablespoons butter, melted

½ cup water

Maple syrup, to taste

1 Preheat the oven to 350°F.

2 Peel the apples, leaving a ring of peel on the bottom where the apple will stand in the skillet. Get as much of the core out as you can without cutting the apple in half.

3 Place the butter in a baking dish. Place the apples bottom-down in the dish. Add the water from the center so that it distributes evenly around the apples. Drizzle the tops of the apples with maple syrup.

4 Put the dish in the oven and cook for about 20 minutes, or until apples are soft. Drizzle with additional maple syrup if desired.

Pineapple Upside-Down Cake

SERVINGS: 8 TO 10 • ACTIVE TIME: 1 HOUR • TOTAL TIME: 2 HOURS

This classic dessert captures the sharp taste of pineapple within sweet, moist cake.

INGREDIENTS

- 8 tablespoons butter, chilled
- 1 (18 oz.) can pineapple rings, plus juice
- ½ cup dark brown sugar
- Maraschino cherries (optional)
- 1 cup light brown sugar
- 2 eggs
- 1 cup buttermilk
- 1 teaspoon vanilla extract
- 1½ cups flour
- 1½ teaspoons baking powder
- ½ teaspoon salt

1 Preheat the oven to 350°F.

2 Heat a cast-iron skillet over medium-high heat. Add 4 tablespoons of the butter. Stir in the juice from the jar of pineapples and the dark brown sugar. Stir continuously while the sugar melts, and continue stirring until the liquid boils and starts to thicken. Cook until the sauce turns a thick, dark, caramel-like consistency.

3 Remove from heat and place the pineapple rings in the liquid, working from the outside in. If using, place a cherry in each ring. Put the skillet in the oven while preparing the batter.

4 To make the cake, beat the remaining butter and light brown sugar with an electric mixer until light and creamy. Beat in the eggs one at a time, making sure the first is thoroughly mixed in before adding the next. Add the buttermilk.

5 In a small bowl, whisk together the flour, baking powder, and salt. Add to the butter-and-sugar mixture.

6 Remove the skillet from the oven and pour the batter over the pineapple rings. Replace in the oven and bake for 45 minutes until cake is golden and a knife inserted in the middle comes out clean.

7 Take the skillet out of the oven and let it rest for about 10 minutes.

8 Find a plate that is an inch or two larger than the top of the skillet and place it over the top. You will be inverting the cake onto the plate. Be sure to use oven mitts or secure pot holders, as the skillet will be hot. Holding the plate tightly against the top of the skillet, turn the skillet over so the plate is now on the bottom. If some of the pineapple is stuck to the bottom, gently remove it and place it on the cake.

9 Allow to cool a few more minutes, or set aside until ready to serve.

Bread Pudding

SERVINGS: 8 TO 10 • ACTIVE TIME: 1 HOUR • TOTAL TIME: 2 HOURS

Bread pudding is a great way to use up slightly stale bread and get a great dessert out of the deal.

1 Prepare a cast-iron skillet by coating it with 2 tablespoons of the butter. Make a layer of bread cubes using half the baguette. Sprinkle half of the raisins, nuts, and fruit over the cubes, and then make another layer, starting with the bread cubes and topping with the raisins, nuts, and fruit.

2 In a large bowl, whisk the eggs until frothy and add the milk, cream, sugar, vanilla, and spices. Whisk briskly to blend thoroughly. Pour the mixture over the bread layers, shaking the pan slightly to be sure to distribute throughout and so that the top cubes are just moistened while the bottom layer gets most of the liquid.

3 Refrigerate for about an hour, pressing down on the bread occasionally.

4 Preheat the oven to 325°F and position a rack in the center. Before putting the skillet in the oven, cut up the remaining 4 tablespoons of butter into little pieces and sprinkle them over the top of the pudding. Bake in the oven for 1 hour.

5 Remove and allow to cool for about 30 minutes. Serve with fresh whipped cream, ice cream, or a Grand Marnier Sauce (see opposite).

Grand Marnier Sauce

BREAD PUDDING INGREDIENTS

6 tablespoons butter

1 large baguette, preferably a day old

¼ cup raisins

⅔ cup toasted almonds or walnuts

1 cup apples or pears, cored and diced

3 eggs

1½ cups milk

1½ cups heavy cream

1 cup sugar

1 tablespoon vanilla extract

¼ teaspoon cinnamon

⅛ teaspoon nutmeg

⅛ teaspoon ginger

1 Melt the butter in a heavy-bottomed saucepan over medium heat. Add the sugar and stir constantly with a wooden spoon while it dissolves and begins to cook. Stir until dissolved, about 2 minutes, then stir in the Grand Marnier, continue to cook for a minute or 2, and remove from the heat.

2 In a bowl, whisk the egg until frothy. Add a large spoonful of the warm Grand Marnier-and-sugar mixture to the egg and continue to whisk so that it combines. Transfer this to the saucepan and whisk it in with the rest of the sauce.

3 On low heat, cook the sauce, whisking constantly, until it starts to thicken, about 3 minutes. Remove from the heat and continue to whisk as it thickens. Drizzle it over bread pudding, or serve on the side.

GRAND MARNIER SAUCE INGREDIENTS

6 tablespoons butter

½ cup sugar

½ cup Grand Marnier

1 egg

INGREDIENTS

6 Granny Smith apples, peeled, cored, and sliced

1 teaspoon ground cinnamon

¾ cup sugar

1 teaspoon fresh-squeezed lemon juice

1 tablespoon butter

1 tablespoon light brown sugar

2 12-inch piecrusts

1 egg white

Apple Pie

A turkey dinner doesn't feel complete until it's followed by this American classic.

1 Preheat the oven to 350°F.

2 In a large bowl, toss apples with cinnamon, sugar, and lemon juice.

3 Put a cast-iron skillet over medium heat and melt the butter in it. Add the brown sugar and cook, stirring constantly, until sugar is dissolved, 1 or 2 minutes. Carefully remove pan from heat.

4 Place 1 of the piecrusts over the sugar mixture. Fill with the apple mixture, and place the other crust over the apples, crimping the edges together.

5 Brush the top crust with the egg white. Cut 4 or 5 slits in the center.

6 Put the skillet in the oven and bake for about 1 hour until golden brown and bubbly. Cover the outermost edge with aluminum foil in the last 10 minutes of baking to prevent it from burning.

7 Remove from oven and allow to cool before serving.

Blueberry Pie

This pie can either cap a great summer day or transport you back to one.

INGREDIENTS

- 4 cups fresh or frozen blueberries
- 1 tablespoon lemon juice
- 1 cup sugar
- 3 tablespoons flour
- 8 tablespoons butter
- 1 cup light brown sugar
- 2 12-inch piecrusts
- 1 egg white
- 2 tablespoons sugar

1 Preheat the oven to 350°F.

2 If using frozen blueberries, it's not necessary to thaw them completely. Put the blueberries in a large bowl, add the lemon juice, sugar, and flour. Stir to combine.

3 Put a cast-iron skillet over medium heat and melt the butter in it. Add the brown sugar and cook, stirring constantly, until sugar is dissolved, 1 or 2 minutes. Remove pan from heat.

4 Gently place one crust over the sugar mixture. Fill with the blueberry mixture, and place the other crust over the filling, crimping the edges together.

5 Brush the top crust with the egg white, and sprinkle the sugar over it. Cut 4 or 5 slits in the middle.

6 Put the skillet in the oven and bake for 50 to 60 minutes until golden brown and bubbly. Cover the outermost edge with aluminum foil in the last 10 minutes of baking to prevent it from burning.

7 Remove from oven and allow to cool before serving.

NOTE: If you feel like adding a decorative touch to your pie, cut your second pie crust into strips and lay them across the top in a criss-cross pattern!

NOTES:

You can substitute fresh blueberries, blackberries, or even strawberries for the raspberries.

For added texture and crunch, sprinkle polenta over the top of the cake before putting it in the oven.

Add ¼ cup dried organic coconut and an additional ¼ cup of milk. Or substitute unsweetened almond milk for the regular milk.

You can substitute vanilla almond milk for the milk, adding ¼ cup more and omitting the maple syrup (vanilla almond milk is sweet).

Raspberry Corn Cake

The polenta in this cake gives it great texture and makes it tastier too. It also gives the cake a lovely yellow color that highlights the raspberries.

1 Preheat the oven to 350°F. Put a cast-iron skillet in the oven as it warms.

2 In a bowl, mix the flour, polenta, baking powder, baking soda, and salt. In another bowl, whisk together the milk and syrup. Stir the wet ingredients into the dry ingredients and combine thoroughly, taking care not to overmix.

3 Using oven mitts or potholders, remove the hot skillet from the oven and add the pieces of butter. Pour the batter over the butter, and sprinkle the raspberries on top.

4 Put the skillet back in the oven and bake for about 20 minutes, until and a toothpick inserted in the middle comes out clean. Serve with additional berries.

INGREDIENTS

½ cup flour

½ cup finely ground polenta

½ teaspoon baking powder

¼ teaspoon baking soda

¼ teaspoon salt

½ cup milk

¼ cup maple syrup

4 tablespoons butter, cut into pieces

½ cup fresh raspberries

Sweet Potato Candies

YIELD: 20 CANDIES • ACTIVE TIME: 45 MINUTES • TOTAL TIME: 2 TO 4 HOURS

These candies are perfect for when the air is cold and the leaves are as orange as the potatoes. While the nutmeg adds a nice, rich flavor to these candies, you can season them however you like.

INGREDIENTS

1 lb. sweet potatoes

¼ cup honey

Zest of 1 lime

¼ cup freshly-squeezed lime juice

½ teaspoon sea salt

¼ teaspoon freshly ground nutmeg

2 cups sugar

1 cup water

Powdered sugar, for dusting

1 To cook the sweet potatoes, poke a few holes in them with a fork. Microwave on high for 8 to 10 minutes, or until the inside is tender. You may want to flip the potatoes once or twice as they cook. When sweet potatoes are cooked, let stand until cool enough to handle.

2 Scoop out the insides of the potatoes and puree in a blender or food processor. Add the honey, lime zest, lime juice, salt, and nutmeg and stir until combined.

3 Place sugar and water in a saucepan and warm over medium heat until a candy thermometer reads approximately 255°F. Remove from heat and let stand for 1 minute.

4 Gently stir the sweet potato mixture into the pan containing the syrup. Once combined, cook over medium heat until the mixture is thick enough that you can run a spoon through it and leave a canal. Remove from heat. Line a baking sheet with wax paper. Pour contents of pan onto baking sheet so that it rests evenly. Let cool.

5 Once cooled completely, dust the knife, your hands, and cutting surface with powdered sugar to prevent sticking. Cut the candy in to small, ½-inch pieces.

6 Serve immediately or wrap each candy in a little piece of parchment paper and twist both ends in opposite directions to seal.

NOTE: Spices like cinnamon, allspice, cayenne pepper, cardamom, or shredded coconut

Honey Peanut Truffles

There is no better combo than chocolate, peanut butter, and honey. It's the perfect mix of sweet and salty.

INGREDIENTS

1 cup rolled oats

½ cup peanut butter

¼ cup honey

¼ teaspoon sea salt

¼ cup semi-sweet chocolate chips

1 In a food processor, grind the oats until they are very fine. Add the peanut butter, honey, and salt and blend until well combined. Line a baking sheet with parchment paper, scoop out teaspoon-sized balls of the peanut butter mixture, and place on the sheet. Place the sheet into refrigerator for 1 hour.

2 Place chocolate chips in a microwave-safe bowl and microwave for 15 to 20 seconds, or until the chocolate is melted. Mix until smooth, and then remove the baking sheet from the refrigerator. Drizzle the chocolate over the truffles or dip the truffles halfway into the chocolate. Place truffles back into the refrigerator until the chocolate is set.

Dutch Apple Baby

SERVINGS: 4 • ACTIVE TIME: 45 MINUTES • TOTAL TIME: 75 MINUTES

This is a classic cast-iron skillet recipe for an apple pastry that puffs in the oven.

1 Preheat the oven to 425° F and position a rack in the middle.

2 Peel and core the apples. Heat a skillet over medium-high heat. Add the butter and apples and cook, stirring, for 3 to 4 minutes until the apples soften. Add the ¼ cup of sugar and the cinnamon and continue cooking for another 3 or 4 minutes. Distribute the apples evenly over the bottom of the skillet and remove from heat.

3 In a large bowl, mix the remaining sugar, flour, and salt together. In a smaller bowl, whisk together the milk, eggs, and vanilla or almond extract. Add the wet ingredients to the dry ingredients and stir to combine. Pour the batter over the apples.

4 Put the skillet in the oven and bake for 15 to 20 minutes until puffy and browned on the top.

5 Remove the skillet from the oven and allow to cool for a few minutes. Run a knife along the edge of the skillet to loosen the dessert. Put a plate over the skillet and, using oven mitts or pot holders, flip the skillet over so the dessert transfers to the plate. Serve warm with a dusting of confectioners' sugar.

INGREDIENTS

2 firm, semi-tart apples, like Mutsu or Golden Delicious, peeled, cored, and cut into slices

4 tablespoons butter

¼ cup sugar, plus 3 tablespoons

1 tablespoon cinnamon

¾ cup flour

¼ teaspoon salt

¾ cup milk

4 eggs

1 teaspoon vanilla or almond extract

Confectioners' sugar for dusting

Bananas Foster

As elegant as it is delicious, Bananas Foster is a New Orleans classic. It's great fun (and a fabulous spectacle) to light this dessert on fire, and the intense heat caramelizes the butter and rum on the bananas!

INGREDIENTS

3 ripe bananas

6 tablespoons butter

½ cup brown sugar, packed

½ teaspoon cinnamon

¼ cup dark rum

Vanilla ice cream

Pecans, chopped (optional)

Mint leaves (optional)

1 Peel the bananas and cut them in half lengthwise.

2 Heat the skillet over medium-high heat and add the butter, cooking until it melts. Add the brown sugar and cinnamon and stir until incorporated.

3 Lay the banana pieces on the bubbling butter mixture and let cook for about 2 minutes per side. When the bananas are soft and coated with the butter, pour the rum over them. Swirl the rum around in the pan and light it on fire. The flame will burn for a minute or so as the alcohol burns off. When the flame dies down, the dessert is ready.

4 Put the bananas on plates with a scoop of vanilla ice cream, or put the ice cream over them in the skillet and eat out of it. If desired, top with chopped pecans and mint leaves.

Cherry Clafoutis

There is some debate about whether the pits should be removed from the cherries before baking, but even Julia Child left them in, on the belief that they add flavor.

INGREDIENTS

8 tablespoons butter, melted

½ cup, plus 2 teaspoons sugar

⅔ cup flour

½ teaspoon salt

1 teaspoon vanilla extract

3 eggs, beaten

1 cup milk

3 cups ripe cherries (pits in)

Confectioners' sugar, for garnish

1 Preheat the oven to 400°F.

2 In a large bowl, mix together 6 tablespoons of the butter, the sugar, flour, salt, vanilla, eggs, and milk until all ingredients are blended and smooth. Set aside.

3 Put the remaining butter in a cast-iron skillet and put it in the oven to warm up.

4 Transfer the skillet to the stovetop and add the additional butter. Once melted, put the sugar in the skillet and shake it so it distributes evenly. Add the cherries. Pour the batter over the cherries, sprinkle with the reamining sugar, and put the skillet back in the oven. Bake for about 30 minutes, or until the topping is golden brown and set in the center.

5 Sprinkle with confectioners' sugar. Serve warm—and be sure to let diners know that the cherries contain their pits.

Pear Clafoutis

NOTE: Although clafoutis is most delicious served warm, it is plenty tasty served at room temperature or even chilled.

Using almond extract instead of the traditional vanilla extract enhances the nutty quality of the pears in this fun spin on a French dessert.

INGREDIENTS

1 Preheat oven to 400°F.

2 In a large bowl, mix together 6 tablespoons of the butter, sugar, flour, salt, almond extract, eggs, and milk until all ingredients are blended and smooth. Set the batter aside.

3 Put 2 tablespoons of butter in a cast-iron skillet and put it in the oven to heat up.

4 Place another skillet over medium-high heat and add the remaining butter, pears, and ½ cup of sugar. Cook, while stirring, until the pears are just soft and glazed, about 3 minutes.

5 Remove the skillet from the oven and pour in half the batter. Spoon the cooked pears over the batter. Then add the remaining batter. Sprinkle with the 2 teaspons of sugar.

6 Bake in the oven for 25 to 30 minutes until the clafoutis is golden brown and set in the center. Serve warm with whipped cream or confectioners' sugar, if desired.

12 tablespoons butter, melted

½ cup sugar

⅔ cup flour

½ teaspoon salt

1 teaspoon almond extract

3 eggs

1 cup milk

4 pears

½ cup sugar, plus 2 teaspoons

Whipped cream or confectioners' sugar (optional)

Leftovers

The Ultimate Thanksgiving Leftovers Sandwich

SERVINGS: 2 • ACTIVE TIME: 15 MINUTES • TOTAL TIME: 30 MINUTES

This leftover Thanksgiving sandwich is simple and focuses on iconic ingredients to make the whole thing come together.

1 Mix mayonnaise and gravy in a small bowl and season with salt and pepper. Set aside.

2 Place a pan over medium heat and add the oil.

3 Butter your bread slices on one side and spread the gravy-and-mayo mixture over the other. Place turkey, stuffing, and cranberry sauce on top of the gravy-and-mayonnaise spread.

4 Form into sandwiches and cook in the pan until golden brown. Flip and cook the other side until golden brown.

INGREDIENTS

1 tablespoon mayonnaise

1 tablespoon giblet gravy (see page 82)

Salt and pepper, to taste

1 tablespoon canola oil

4 slices of bread

1 tablespoon unsalted butter

Leftover turkey

1 tablespoon cranberry sauce (leftover homemade preferable)

¼ cup preferred stuffing

Homestyle Turkey and Wild Rice Soup

SERVINGS: 5 TO 7 • ACTIVE TIME: 30 MINUTES • TOTAL TIME: 2 HOURS

Combining the homemade turkey stock with perfectly prepared turkey creates a classic cold-weather soup perfect for the day after Thanksgiving.

INGREDIENTS

2 quarts homemade turkey stock (see page 86)

1 lb. leftover turkey

3 carrots, peeled and cut into 1-inch pieces

3 celery stalks, cut into 1-inch pieces

Salt and pepper, to taste

4 sprigs thyme

5 garlic cloves, minced

1 medium onion, diced

1 cup wild rice

1 Add all of the ingredients except the rice to a large stockpot.

2 Bring to a boil, then reduce heat to simmer for 1 hour, or until liquid is reduced by a third.

3 Add the rice. Cook until the rice is tender, about 20 minutes.

Chickpea and Leftover Turkey Chili

SERVINGS: 5 TO 7 • ACTIVE TIME: 35 MINUTES
TOTAL TIME: 2 HOURS AND 35 MINUTES

While chili isn't always the first use for leftover turkey, this spicy combination is sure to make a lasting impression.

CHICKPEA AND LEFTOVER TURKEY CHILI INGREDIENTS

- 1 tablespoon olive oil
- 1 medium onion, diced
- 5 garlic cloves, minced
- 1 tablespoon fresh oregano, chopped
- Black pepper, to taste
- 1 tablespoon cumin
- 2 teaspoons chili powder
- 2 cups turkey stock (see page 86)
- 8 oz. tomatoes (canned or fresh)
- 3 dried New Mexico chilies
- 1 red bell pepper, seeded and diced
- Pinch of salt
- 1 (15.5 oz.) can of chickpeas
- 1 lb. leftover turkey
- 2 cups cheddar cheese, shredded (optional)
- 1 cup sour cream (optional)

CHICKPEA AND LEFTOVER TURKEY CHILI DIRECTIONS

1 Place olive oil in a Dutch oven and place it over medium-high heat.

2 Add onion, garlic, oregano, pepper, cumin, and chili powder. Cook for 5 minutes, stirring often.

3 Add turkey stock, tomatoes, New Mexico chilies, bell pepper, salt, chickpeas, and turkey.

4 Stir the mixture, cover, and reduce the heat to low. Cook for 2 hours, stirring occasionally.

5 Scoop chili into bowls and top with cheese and sour cream, if desired.

with **Cornbread and Rosemary Butter**

ROSEMARY BUTTER INGREDIENTS

2 sprigs rosemary

4 tablespoons unsalted butter at room temperature

Pinch of salt

ROSEMARY BUTTER DIRECTIONS

1 Mince the rosemary.

2 Place the butter, salt, and rosemary in a bowl and beat until light and fluffy.

3 Place the whipped butter in a container and refrigerate until needed.

CORNBREAD INGREDIENTS

2 large eggs

1½ cups milk

5 tablespoons butter, melted

1 cup cornmeal

¾ cup all-purpose flour

1 tablespoon sugar

1 teaspoon baking powder

½ teaspoon baking soda

Pinch of salt

CORNBREAD DIRECTIONS

1 Preheat the oven to 450°F.

2 Grease an 8 x 8–inch baking dish.

3 In a small bowl, combine the eggs, milk, and butter.

4 In a large bowl, combine the cornmeal, flour, sugar, baking powder, baking soda, and salt.

5 Combine the wet and dry mixtures and mix together until there are no lumps.

6 Pour the batter into the greased baking dish and bake until the top is brown and the middle is set, about 20 to 25 minutes.

7 Remove from the oven and let cool completely. Serve with Rosemary Butter.

METRIC CONVERSION CHART

US MEASUREMENT	APPROXIMATE METRIC LIQUID MEASUREMENT	APPROXIMATE METRIC DRY MEASUREMENT
1 teaspoon	5 mL	
1 tablespoon or ½ ounce	15 mL	14 g
1 ounce or ⅛ cup	30 mL	28 g
¼ cup or 2 ounces	60 mL	57 g
⅓ cup	80 mL	
½ cup or 4 ounces	120 mL	113 g
⅔ cup	160 mL	
¾ cup or 6 ounces	180 mL	
1 cup or 8 ounces or ½ pint	240 mL	227 g
1½ cups or 12 ounces	350 mL	
2 cups or 1 pint or 16 ounces	475 mL	453 g
3 cups or 1½ pints	700 mL	
4 cups or 2 pints or 1 quart	950 mL	

ABOUT THE AUTHOR

CHEF KEITH SARASIN's love for food was developed at a young age when he would cook for his mother using old cookbooks given to him by his grandmother. He began his culinary career at the age of 15, washing dishes and making subs at a sandwich shop. As the years went on he worked his way from sous chef to executive chef. Sarasin worked as a private chef before founding The Farmers Dinner, a farm-to-table event planning company. The Farmers Dinner concept came from Sarasin's time working with farms in New England. He wanted a way to support local farms while sharing the stories he learned from spending time with various farmers. In 2012, he launched the first Farmers Dinner in Nashua, New Hampshire. It quickly sold out and subsequent events followed. Since 2012, The Farmers Dinner has hosted over 60 farm-to-table dinners on farms across New England, fed more than 6,000 customers, and raised over $74,000 for local farms.

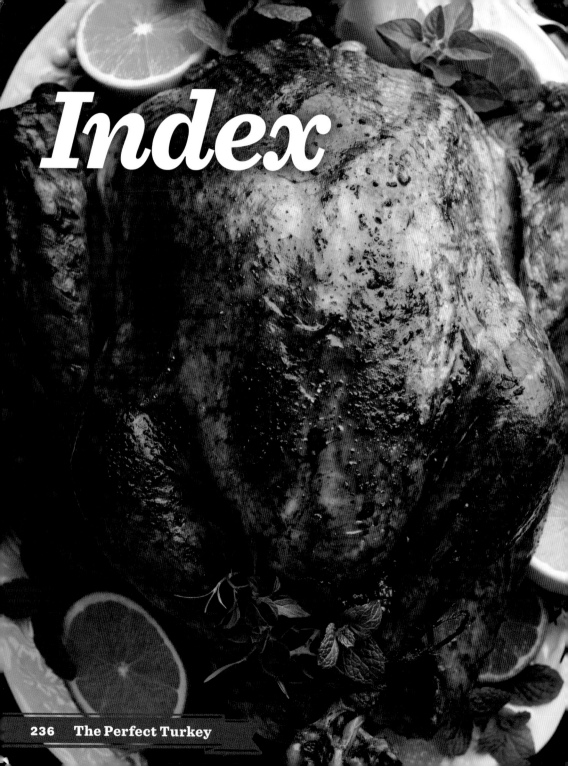

Index

About Cider Mill Press Book Publishers

Good ideas ripen with time. From seed to harvest, Cider Mill Press
brings fine reading, information, and entertainment together between
the covers of its creatively crafted books. Our Cider Mill bears fruit twice
a year, publishing a new crop of titles each spring and fall.